Enfield Libra

Branch:

# TEST AND ASSESS YOUR BRAIN QUOTIENT

# TEST AND ASSESS YOUR BRAIN QUOTIENT

Discover your true intelligence with tests of aptitude, logic, memory, EQ, creative and lateral thinking

**PHILIP CARTER**

London and Philadelphia

**Publisher's note**

Every possible effort has been made to ensure that the information contained in this book is accurate at the time of going to press, and the publishers and author cannot accept responsibility for any errors or omissions, however caused. No responsibility for loss or damage occasioned to any person acting, or refraining from action, as a result of the material in this publication can be accepted by the editor, the publisher or the author.

First published in Great Britain and the United States in 2009 by Kogan Page Limited

Apart from any fair dealing for the purposes of research or private study, or criticism or review, as permitted under the Copyright, Designs and Patents Act 1988, this publication may only be reproduced, stored or transmitted, in any form or by any means, with the prior permission in writing of the publishers, or in the case of reprographic reproduction in accordance with the terms and licences issued by the CLA. Enquiries concerning reproduction outside these terms should be sent to the publishers at the undermentioned addresses:

120 Pentonville Road          525 South 4th Street, #241
London N1 9JN                 Philadelphia PA 19147
United Kingdom                USA
www.koganpage.com

© Philip Carter, 2009

The right of Philip Carter to be identified as the author of this work has been asserted by him in accordance with the Copyright, Designs and Patents Act 1988.

ISBN 978 0 7494 5416 6

---

**British Library Cataloguing-in-Publication Data**

A CIP record for this book is available from the British Library.

---

**Library of Congress Cataloging-in-Publication Data**

Carter, Philip J.
    Test and assess your brain quotient / Philip Carter.
        p. cm.
    ISBN 978-0-7494-5416-6
    1. Intelligence tests. I. Title.
    BF431.3.C3725 2008
    153.9'3--dc22
                                                2008028276

---

| London Borough of Enfield | | |
|---|---|---|
| 91200000022637 | | |
| Askews | | Dec-2008 |
| 153.93 | | £8.99 |
| AnF | | 1/09 |

Typeset by Saxon Graphics Ltd, Derby
Printed and bound in India by Replika Press Pvt Ltd

# Contents

|   | | |
|---|---|---|
| | Introduction | 1 |
| 1 | **IQ testing** | 5 |
| | Test one: IQ test | 6 |
| | Answers | 21 |
| 2 | **Agility of mind** | 25 |
| | Test one: speed test – true or false | 25 |
| | Test two: verbal dexterity test | 28 |
| | Test three: eclectic agility of mind test | 30 |
| | Test four: find the letter test | 34 |
| | Test five: word and letter arrangement test | 36 |
| | Answers | 38 |
| | Agility of mind: overall assessment | 42 |
| 3 | **Tests of logical analysis** | 43 |
| | Test one: general test | 44 |
| | Test two: progressive numerical matrix test | 53 |
| | Test three: symbolic complete the sequence test | 68 |
| | Answers | 72 |
| | Tests of logical analysis: overall assessment | 76 |

## 4 Tests of numerical aptitude — 77
Test one: sequences — 77
Test two: mental arithmetic test — 81
Test three: complete the equation test — 84
Test four: general numerical test — 89
Answers — 96
Tests of numerical aptitude: overall assessment — 102

## 5 Tests of spatial aptitude — 103
Test one: box clever test — 104
Test two: general test — 114
Answers — 123
Tests of spatial aptitude: overall assessment — 125

## 6 Personality questionnaires — 127
Test one: attitude — 128
Test two: success factor — 135
Test three: how imaginative are you? — 142
Answers — 149
Personality questionnaires: overall assessment — 153

## 7 Tests and exercises of creative thinking — 155

### Part 1: tests of creative thinking — 157
Test one: (symbolic) odd one out test — 157
Test two: find the missing symbol test — 160
Test three: diagrammatic find the link test — 165
Answers — 166
Tests of creative thinking: overall assessment — 168

### Part 2: exercises of creative thinking — 169
Exercise one: left-/right-brain thinking personality test — 171
Exercise two: imaginative shapes — 173
Exercise three: the bucket test — 175

| 8 | Memory | **177** |
|---|---|---|
|   | Memory tests | 179 |
| 9 | **Tests of verbal aptitude** | **203** |
|   | Test one: synonym test | 203 |
|   | Test two: antonym test | 209 |
|   | Test three: synonym and antonym test | 215 |
|   | Test four: lexical ability test | 216 |
|   | Answers | 222 |
|   | Tests of verbal aptitude: overall assessment | 225 |
| 10 | **Overall BQ rating and assessment** | **227** |

# *Introduction*

As well as providing valuable brain training material, the primary purpose of this book is to include tests for several different types of intelligence and, in the concluding chapter, collate the results into a final assessment to produce an overall brain quotient (BQ) rating.

The book is divided into several chapters, with each chapter testing and assessing a different aspect of intelligence: IQ, agility of mind, logical analysis, numerical aptitude, spatial aptitude, EQ (personality), creative thinking, memory and verbal aptitude.

In addition to obtaining an overall BQ rating, readers can, because of the way the book is structured, identify their own particular strengths and weaknesses. They have, therefore, the opportunity to build on their strengths and work at improving their performance in areas of weakness.

Whilst the providing of an overall BQ rating is an innovative new concept, it has been argued for some time that the traditional method of intelligence measurement, the IQ test, is too narrow as a definition of intelligence.

IQ tests assess only what is termed as general ability in three categories of intelligence: numerical, verbal and spatial (abstract) reasoning. However, there are several other equally important and valuable types of intelligence that need to be recognized and developed.

Scores from standardized intelligence tests (IQ scores) are widely used to define one's intelligence level. It is, however, becoming increasingly apparent, and accepted, that they do not reveal the complete picture and provide only a snapshot of a person's ability in the area under examination. For example, someone who has scored highly on a verbal test can only be said to have a high verbal IQ, and someone who has scored highly on a mathematical test can only be said to have a high numerical IQ. Obviously, therefore, the more different types of disciplines that are tested and examined, the more accurately the intelligence level of the individual can be assessed.

The concept of *general intelligence*, or *g*, was devised in the early 20th century by the English psychologist Charles Spearman, who established *g* as a measure of performance in a variety of tests.

Spearman's research led him to the conclusion that the same people who performed well in a variety of mental tasks tended to use a part of the brain that he termed *g*. The *g* factor, therefore, laid the foundation for the concept of a single intelligence, and the belief that this single, and measurable, intelligence enables us to perform tasks of mental ability.

As we learn more about the workings of the human brain, Spearman's concept has become highly controversial and is increasingly challenged by those who claim that the concept of a single overall intelligence is too simplistic.

To cite just one example of this, we know now, as a result of work carried out in the 1960s by the US neurologist Roger Wolcott Sperry (1913–94), that the creative functions of human beings are controlled by the right-hand hemisphere of the human brain. This is the side of the brain that is underused by the majority of people, as opposed to the thought processes of the left-hand hemisphere, which is characterized by order, sequence and logic and is responsible for such functions as numerical and verbal skills.

In addition there is increasing recognition of the importance of the concept of emotional intelligence developed in the mid-1990s by Daniel Goleman, and the theory of multiple intelligences in which Howard Gardner, a professor of education at Harvard University, defines intelligence as the potential ability to process a certain sort of information. The different types of intelligence are for the most part independent of one another, and no type is more important than the others.

Whilst intelligence quotient (IQ) tests are, and will remain, helpful in predicting future performance or potential in many areas (in recognition of this a 50-question IQ test has been included in the first chapter of this book and forms part of the overall BQ assessment), they do not provide us with other information, such as that about the ability to connect with other people emotionally or the performing of creative tasks that involve the use of imagination.

By expanding our definition of intelligence to include multiple intelligences we can identify, appreciate and nurture more of our strengths. This is important, as it would be as rare for any one individual to be endowed in all the different intelligences as it would for any one individual not to possess some kind of talent. We all tend to be aware of some of our abilities and limitations, for instance some of us may be capable of producing great works of art but completely hopeless when it comes to fixing a problem with the plumbing; others who may be championship-class chess players would never be able to smash a tennis ball into the opposing player's court; and others may possess great linguistic skills but feel completely at a loss trying to make small talk at social gatherings. The fact is that no one is talented in every domain and no one is completely incapable in every domain.

The main lesson to be learned from this is that people can be intelligent in many different ways. It is completely wrong to write off or even put down someone who has scored badly in an IQ test, which after all has provided us with only one type of information about that individual. All of us have the potential for achievement in some kind of intelligence, and we also possess the potential for improvement in many other areas.

## How to assess your brain quotient

At the end of the answers to each individual test a performance indicator is provided. Scores from each of these tests may then be transferred to the overall assessment charts at the end of the chapters in order to obtain an overall assessment for each type of intelligence.

The total scores from each chapter may then be transferred to the overall BQ rating chart in Chapter 10 on page 227, from which you can then obtain your final brain quotient (BQ) rating factor.

# IQ testing

The 50 questions in the following IQ test are multidisciplinary. They are designed to test verbal, numerical and spatial (diagrammatic) aptitudes in approximately equal measure, together with a degree of creative and lateral thinking.

Of the different methods that purport to measure intelligence, the most famous is the intelligence quotient (IQ) test, which is a standardized test designed to measure human intelligence as distinct from attainments. Usually, IQ tests consist of a graded series of tasks, each of which has been standardized with a large representative population of individuals in order to establish an average IQ of 100 for each test.

Like so many distributions found in nature, the distribution of IQ takes the form of a fairly regular bell curve in which the average score is 100 and similar proportions occur both above and below this norm.

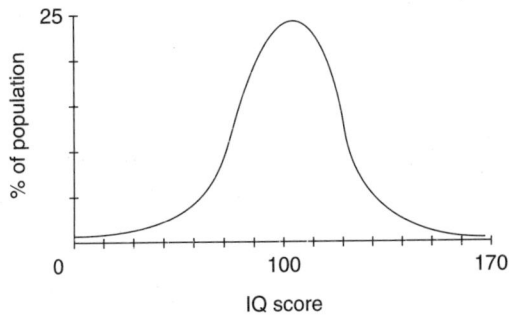

# Test one: IQ test

*Instructions:*
A time limit of 120 minutes is allowed for the completion of all 50 questions. You should keep strictly to this time limit; otherwise your assessment rating will be invalidated.

The use of calculators is not permitted in respect of the numerical questions, which are designed to test your aptitude when working with numbers as well as your powers of mental arithmetic.

*Note:*
This test has been specially compiled for this book; it has not, therefore, been standardized, so an actual IQ assessment cannot be given. However, a guide to assessing your performance is provided, the score of which will contribute to your overall BQ rating.

1.

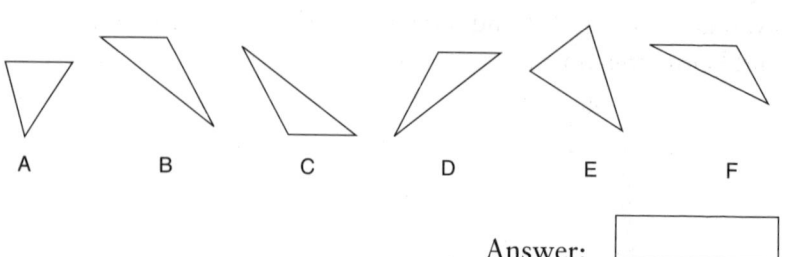

Which figure should replace the question mark?

Answer:

2. Which word in brackets is most opposite in meaning to the word in capitals?

   EXPEDITE (dispatch, dismiss, curb, press, conclude)

   Answer:

3. How many minutes is it before noon if 29 minutes ago it was six times as many minutes past 10 am?

   Answer:

4. A    E    G    K    M    ?

   What comes next?

   Answer:

5.

| 2 | 3 | 5 | 8 |
|---|---|---|---|
| 1 | 5 | 6 | 11 |
| 3 | 8 | 11 | 19 |
| 4 | 13 | 17 | ? |

What number should replace the question mark?

Answer:

6. → ♯ Ω ♪ ☼ ♠ — ♯ Ω ♪ ☼ ♠ — Ω ♪ ☼ ♠ —

   Which symbol comes next?

   a.  Ω
   b.  ♯
   c.  ☼
   d.  ♪
   e.  →

   Answer: ☐

7. 473 (50), 578 (65), 529 (?)

   What number should replace the question mark?

   Answer: ☐

8. 

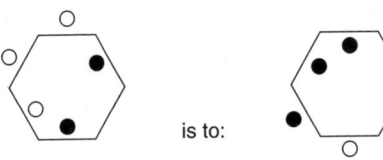

is to: 

as:

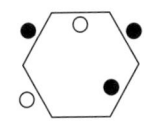

is to:

A 

B 

C 

D 

E 

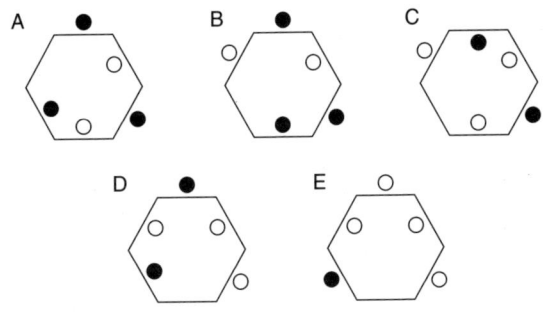

Answer:

9. 639 (33), 584 (37), 965 (39), 868 (?)

What number should replace the question mark?

Answer:

10. Which is the odd one out?

dilate, elaborate, amplify, expatiate, interpret

Answer:

10  Test and assess your brain quotient

11. 7942163987581276

What is the sum of all the odd numbers in the above list that are immediately followed by another odd number?

Answer: [          ]

12.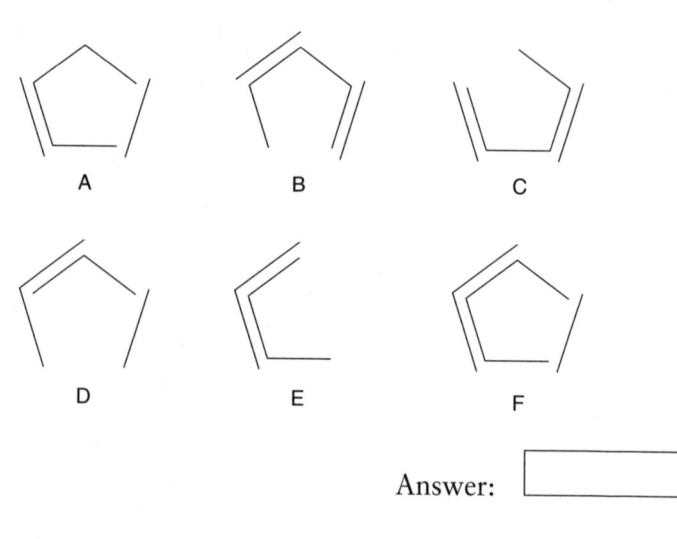

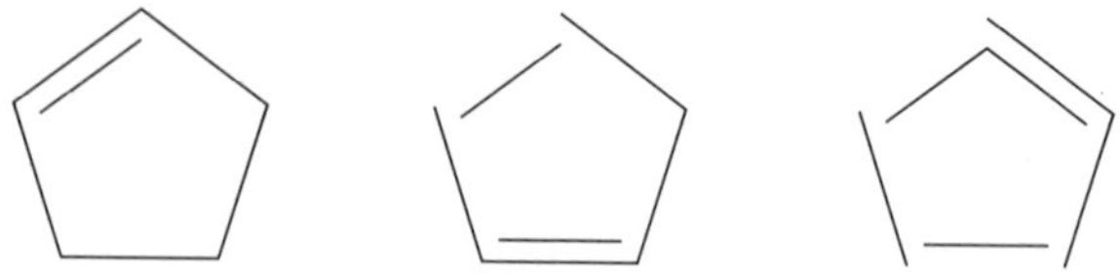

What comes next?

Answer: [          ]

13.  A   B   C   D   E   F   G   H

What letter is three to the left of the letter that is immediately to the right of the letter that is two to the left of the letter F?

Answer: [          ]

14. Which word in brackets is closest in meaning to the word in capitals?

    ESPOUSE (forswear, embrace, elude, amplify, discharge)

    Answer:

15. Insert a word in the brackets so that it completes a word or phrase when tacked on to the word on the left and completes another word or phrase when placed in front of the word on the right.

    FLY (     ) ORAL

    Answer:

16. Which is the odd one out?

    7568    9637    4205    6549    9740

    Answer:

17. ●●□—●●●□□—●●●●□□□—●●●●●□□□□—●●●●

    Which three symbols come next?

    a.  ●●●
    b.  □—●
    c.  ●□—
    d.  ●●□
    e.  ●□□

    Answer:

## Test and assess your brain quotient

18. compartment is to train as fitment is to: offshoot, machine, part, component, facet

    Answer:

19. Z  X  U  Q  L  ?

    What letter should replace the question mark?

    Answer:

20. What numerical value produces the same amount when it is added to 3 as when multiplied by 3?

    Answer:

21. Which option below continues the sequence?

    A  B  C  D  E  F

    Answer:

22. evoke is to arouse as engrave is to:
    preserve, fix, summon, craft, image

    Answer:

23. What word meaning *the preservation of documents and papers* means *throw with force* when a letter is removed?

    Answer:

24. 65, 84, 105, ?, 153, 180

    What number should replace the question mark?

    Answer:

25. Which is the odd one out?

    a. ▼◄▲▼►
    b. ▲◄▼►▲
    c. ►▼▲◄▼
    d. ▼◄►▲▼
    e. ▲►▼◄▲

    Answer:

26. Which is the odd one out?

    canticle, verse, shanty, madrigal, aria

    Answer:

27. A  E  H  J  N  Q  S  ?

What letter should replace the question mark?

Answer: [      ]

28. 7, 22, 67, 202, ?

What number should replace the question mark?

Answer: [      ]

29. 

is to:

as:

is to:

A  B  C  D  E

Answer: [      ]

30. What is the meaning of the word 'approbation'?

    a. conversation
    b. approval
    c. lack of interest
    d. an excess of self-confidence
    e. glorification

Answer: [      ]

31. Jane has £430 to spend. She spends 3/5 of the £430 on new clothes, 0.125 of the £430 on jewellery and a further £10.75 on a meal. What is her financial situation at the end of the day?

Answer:

32. Which is the odd one out?

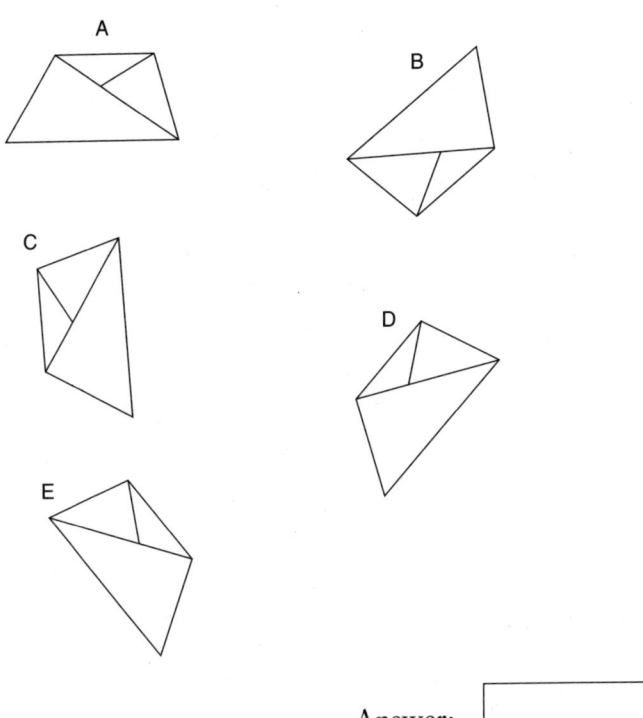

Answer:

33. Which word in brackets is most opposite in meaning to the word in capitals?

SUPERCILIOUS
(morbid, unremarkable, morose, modest, imperious)

Answer:

34. Identify two words (one from each set of brackets) that form a connection to the words in capitals, thereby relating to them in the same way (analogy).

LEER (look, ogle, mock, lust)
GLOWER (inspect, scowl, peer, glance)

Answer:

35. 361 (21), 952 (63), 862 (?)

What number should replace the question mark?

Answer:

36.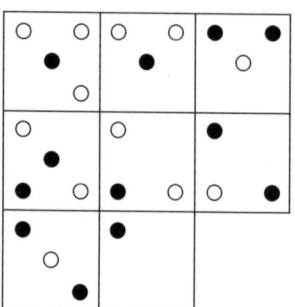

Which is the missing tile?

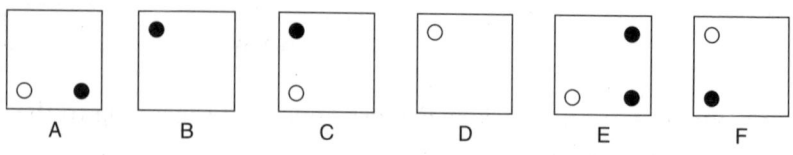

Answer:

37. Which is the odd one out?

   predicament, nostrum, imbroglio, enigma, quagmire

   Answer:

38.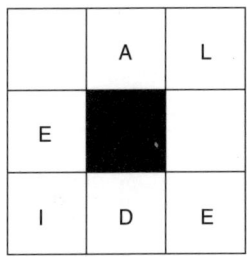

   Find the starting point and spiral clockwise to spell out an eight-letter word. You have to provide the missing letters.

   Answer:

39.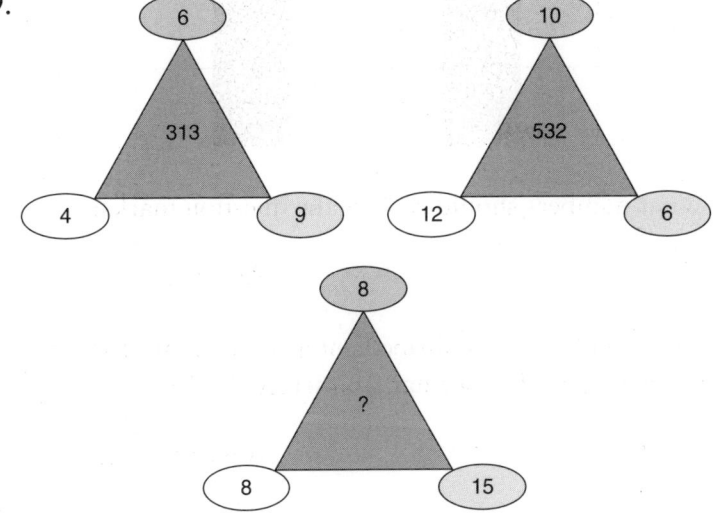

   What number should replace the question mark?

   Answer:

40.

[shape with filled dot upper-left, open circle lower-right on triangle] is to: [inverted triangle with filled dot upper-right, open circle lower-bottom]

as:

[bullet shape with open circle upper, filled dot lower] is to:

A  B  C  D  E  F

Answer: [ ]

41.

| 3 | 11 | ■ | 9 | 23 | ■ | 8 | ? |
|---|----|---|---|----|---|---|---|
| 4 | 7  | ■ | 7 | 16 | ■ | 7 | ? |

What numbers should replace the question marks?

Answer: [ ]

42. non-compliant is to disobedient as non-committed is to: irregular, guarded, secular, uninterested, silent

Answer: [ ]

43. A photograph measuring 4.8 × 6 cm is to be enlarged. If the enlargement of the shorter side is 12.6 cm, what is the length of the longer side?

Answer:

44. Which is the odd one out?

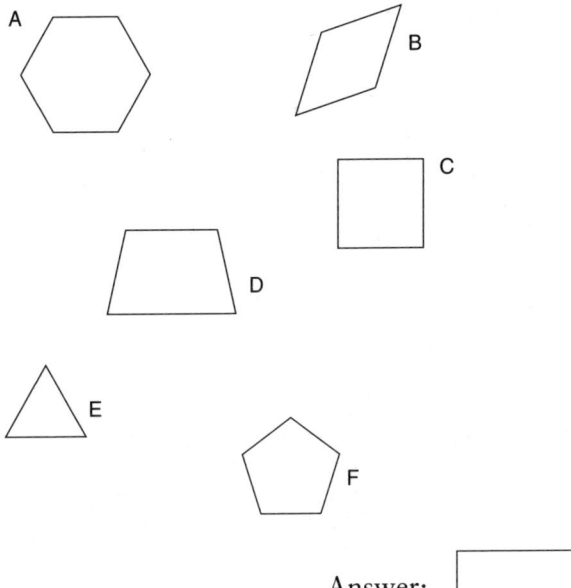

Answer:

45. 1, 2, 5, 10, 13, ?, 29

What number should replace the question mark?

Answer:

46. Solve the one-word anagram in capitals to complete the sentence correctly.

The report provided the necessary KNOW RUG ROD for the research.

Answer:

47. 4936 (76), 8125 (95), 1664 (?)

What number should replace the question mark?

Answer:

48.

What comes next?

A  B  C  D  E

Answer:

49. Which two words are closest in meaning?

amend, secede, conceal, disaffiliate, endorse, inveigle

Answer:

50. What is the lowest fractional value of the following?

3/4 ÷ 9/8

Answer:

## Answers

1. B. The first three figures are being repeated, but upside down.
2. curb
3. 13 minutes
4. Q. The sequence progresses AbcdEfGhijKlMnopQ.
5. 30. In each row and column add the first and second numbers to give the third number and the second and third numbers to obtain the fourth number.
6. d. After each line — the first symbol from the previous set is discarded.
7. 61
   $59 + 2 = 61$
   Similarly: $43 + 7 = 50$ and $58 + 7 = 65$
8. D. Dots outside move to the inside and change colour – and vice versa.
9. 56
   $(6 \times 8) + 8$
   Similarly: $(3 \times 9) + 6 = 33$, $(8 \times 4) + 5 = 37$ and $(6 \times 5) + 9 = 39$
10. interpret: it means 'translate'. The rest mean 'explain in lengthy detail' or 'enlarge upon'.
11. 17 (7 + 3 + 7)
12. A. As the internal pentagon is being constructed line by line, the external pentagon is being disassembled line by line. The same line is removed from the external pentagon that corresponds with the line added to the internal pentagon at the previous stage.
13. B
14. embrace
15. past
    fly-past, pastoral
16. 9740. In all the others multiply the first and last digits to obtain the middle two digits.

17. d. The sequence progresses two black dots/one white square/line, three black dots/two white squares/line, etc.
18. machine
19. F. The sequence progresses ZyXwvUtsrQponmLkjihgF.
20. 1.5
21. C. The line moves 45° anticlockwise at each stage and the black section moves 45° clockwise.
22. fix
23. filing, fling
24. 128. Add 19, 21, 23, 25, 27.
25. d. a has the same symbols as c in reverse and b has the same as e in reverse.
26. verse. The rest are types of songs or singing.
27. W. The sequence progresses AbcdEfgHiJklmNopQrStuvW.
28. 607. Multiply by 3 and add 1 at each stage.
29. D. The figures are mirror images of each other.
30. b
31. She has £107.50 left.
32. E. The rest are the same figure rotated.
33. modest
34. ogle, scowl
35. 64

    8 × (6 + 2)
36. D. The contents of the third tile in each line and column are determined by the contents of the first two tiles. Only when the same coloured dot appears in the same position in the first two tiles is it carried forward to the third tile, where it then changes from black to white and vice versa.
37. nostrum
38. medieval
39. 425. To obtain the first digit (4) divide the top number by 2. To obtain the second digit (2) divide the bottom left number by 4. To obtain the third digit (5) divide the bottom right number by 3.

40. C. The large figure rotates 180°. The dot in the middle goes to the left. The dot at the bottom remains at the bottom.
41. 15 and 22. Working round each square anticlockwise from the top left, the third and fourth numbers are the sum of the previous two numbers.
42. guarded
43. 15.75 cm
    12.6 divided by 4.8 and multiplied by 6
44. D. In all the other figures the sides are the same length.
45. 26
    × 2, + 3, × 2, + 3, etc
46. groundwork
47. 48
    $\sqrt{16} = 4$ and $\sqrt{64} = 8$
48. C. The black dot on the outside is moving 90° anticlockwise at each stage.
49. secede, disaffiliate
50. 2/3

## Assessment

Score 1 point for each correct answer.

| | |
|---|---|
| 16–24 | Average |
| 25–34 | Good |
| 35–44 | Very good |
| 45–50 | Exceptional |

Transfer your score to the overall brain quotient (BQ) rating chart on page 227.

# 2

# Agility of mind

Agility of mind is the ability to think quickly and react instinctively. It is a valuable asset to have at one's disposal in many situations.

All the tests in this chapter are speed tests, where it is necessary to keep calm and maintain your concentration whilst working against the clock.

## Test one: speed test – true or false

*Instructions:*
In this speed test you have to work quickly through a series of 20 statements, maintaining your concentration on just one question at a time throughout, and decide simply whether each statement is TRUE or FALSE.

You have 30 minutes in which to answer the 20 questions.

*Example:*
50 minutes after 12 noon is the same as 70 minutes before 2 pm.

    TRUE or FALSE.

    Answer: TRUE

1. The number 78654321098 written in reverse is 89012354687.

   TRUE or FALSE.

2. 85% of 200 is the same as 34 multiplied by 5.

   TRUE or FALSE.

3. The word MERCHANT can be spelled using all but one of the letters from the word PARCHMENT.

   TRUE or FALSE.

4. This sentence contains the letter 's' just seven times.

   TRUE or FALSE.

5. 200 less 36 is the same as 150 plus 124.

   TRUE or FALSE.

6. The letter H is the same distance from the beginning of the alphabet as the letter S is from the end of the alphabet.

   TRUE or FALSE.

7. When it is 2.45 an upside-down clock's minute hand points to the left.

   TRUE or FALSE.

8. It is possible to make four four-letter English words from the letters AEDR.

   TRUE or FALSE.

9. 369, 468, 567

   The next number in the above sequence is 665.

   TRUE or FALSE.

10. Frank is older than Alan but younger than Barry.
    Alan is younger than Frank but older than Paul.
    Therefore, Paul is the youngest of the four.

    TRUE or FALSE.

11. If you write down all the numbers from 1 to 50 inclusive, you would write the number 5 six times.

    TRUE or FALSE.

12. 15 per cent of 70 is the same as 25 per cent of 42.

    TRUE or FALSE.

13. If I write the word LAD under the word MAN and the word BOY above the word MAN, the word BAD appears reading diagonally.

    TRUE or FALSE.

14. ACFHK

    The letter O should appear next in the above sequence.

    TRUE or FALSE.

15. CAT     COT     ?     DOG

    The word GOT is missing from the above sequence.

    TRUE or FALSE.

16. 18   27   34   72   53   84   28

    Two of the above numbers add up to 100 exactly.

    TRUE or FALSE.

17. 6 May comes 14 days exactly after 22 April.

    TRUE or FALSE.

18. Six lions and three ostriches have a total of 30 legs between them.

    TRUE or FALSE.

19. The number 78521634819 rewritten with all its digits in ascending order is 11234567889.

    TRUE or FALSE.

20. In the alphabet, the letter two before the letter four letters after the letter J is the letter M.

    TRUE or FALSE.

## Test two: verbal dexterity test

You have 90 minutes to try to solve as many of the anagrams as possible. The answers are all one word.

1. LAIDARM

   Answer: ____

2. BOILTAR

   Answer: ____

3. PETSTEM

   Answer: ____

4. SUNCLOT

   Answer: ____

5. SCANBEE

   Answer: ____

6. DOESPIE

   Answer: ____

7. RIPHEAP      Answer:

8. MRTAUNT     Answer:

9. RIOTSUM     Answer:

10. SEWTRAM    Answer:

11. LEDMARE    Answer:

12. BEAMAIL    Answer:

13. ANSHIRT    Answer:

14. RARELIE    Answer:

15. ACEGIRL    Answer:

16. RIBALEC    Answer:

17. CLIPEAR    Answer:

18. TURNARC    Answer:

19. IDOLBAT    Answer:

20. NEATROB    Answer:

21. CANEHIM    Answer:

22. USAMAST    Answer:

23. SUEREID

Answer: [ ]

24. ARTDISC

Answer: [ ]

25. SOFTONE

Answer: [ ]

26. TOURCAR

Answer: [ ]

27. SOMEHUG

Answer: [ ]

28. CORNFEE

Answer: [ ]

29. ARCMICE

Answer: [ ]

30. MEREPRO

Answer: [ ]

## Test three: eclectic agility of mind test

You have 60 minutes in which to answer the 20 questions.

1. If the word SIDE is written under the word BOAR, the word CALM is written above the word BOAR and the word DOME is written under the word SIDE, what word is produced reading diagonally from the top left-hand corner to the bottom right-hand corner?

    Answer: [ ]

2. What day and date is it 36 days after Monday, 10 March?

    Answer: [ ]

3. What is twenty-one thousand, twenty-one hundred and twenty-one less twenty-two thousand, two hundred and twenty-two?

   Answer:

4. A   D   H   M   ?

   What comes next?

   Answer:

5. If I walk 2 miles east, then 1 mile south, then 1 mile east, then 2 miles north and finally 3 miles west, how far am I, and in what direction, from my starting point?

   Answer:

6. 72593176852913462

   Multiply the numbers together that only appear once in the above list.

   Answer:

7. Which is greater, four-fifths of 995 or one-third of 2,385?

   Answer:

8. How many minutes is it before midnight if 15 minutes ago it was twice as many minutes past 10 pm?

   Answer:

9. Write the numbers 365247634635 in reverse, omitting the lowest and highest numbers.

   Answer:

10. S762AC34BK5DN

    Write down all the odd numbers from the above list in ascending order, followed by all the letters in reverse alphabetical order, followed by all the even numbers in descending order.

    Answer:

11. Read and memorize this question very carefully for 20 seconds, then look away from the page and write down the number of times the letter 't' appears.

    Answer:

12. The name of which animal (six letters long) can be produced from the letters of the word MENAGERIE?

    Answer:

13. 2, 5, 10, 17, 26, ?

    What number should replace the question mark?

    Answer:

14. If I have £960 and spend one-third in the morning and then a further £48 in the afternoon, how much am I left with?

    Answer:

15. 629473168274923

    Add together all the odd numbers in the above list that are immediately followed by an even number.

    Answer:

16. B R O L A C F I T

    What word is spelled out by the ninth, second, eighth, first, fifth and fourth letters in the above list?

    Answer:

17. If Tom has one-third, Peter has 40%, Mike has 50% and Naomi has one more than Peter, what percentage has Caroline?

    Answer:

18. 2 3 4 7 1 6 8

    Multiply the second-highest odd number and the second-lowest even number in the above list.

    Answer:

19. What letter in the English alphabet comes four letters before the letter that comes two letters after the letter N?

    Answer:

20. F A Z N T D K L P S K O E T J

    Which are the only two letters that appear twice in the above list?

    Answer:

## Test four: find the letter test

You have 30 minutes in which to answer the 10 questions.

*Questions 1–5:*

| A | B | C | D | E | F | G | H |

1. What letter is two to the left of the letter immediately to the right of the letter D?

   Answer:

2. What letter is immediately to the left of the letter that is three to the right of the letter immediately to the left of the letter D?

   Answer:

3. What letter is midway between the letter that is four to the right of the letter D and the letter two to the left of the letter H?

   Answer:

4. What letter is two to the right of the letter four to the left of the letter that is immediately to the right of the letter E?

   Answer:

5. What letter is immediately to the left of the letter that comes midway between the letter three to the left of the letter D and the letter two to the left of the letter G?

   Answer:

## Questions 6–10:

| A | B | C | D | E |   |
|---|---|---|---|---|---|
| F | G | H | I | J |   |
| K | L | M | N | O |   |
| P | Q | R | S | T |   |
| U | V | W | X | Y | Z |

6. What letter comes two letters below the letter that is three to the right of the letter F?

   Answer:

7. What letter is three above the letter that is two to the left of the letter that is two places below the letter N?

   Answer:

8. What letter is midway between the letter three to the left of the letter S and the letter three places above the letter W?

   Answer:

9. What letter is immediately to the left of the letter two above the letter immediately to the right of the letter two above the letter four to the left of the letter Z?

   Answer:

10. What letter is two to the left of the letter that comes midway between the letter three to the right of the letter W and the letter two below the letter D?

    Answer:

## Test five: word and letter arrangement test

You have 45 minutes in which to answer the 20 questions.

Arrange the letters in alphabetical order followed by the numbers in ascending order.

1. N 8 6 B K L

   Answer:

2. 5 A N D 8 F J T 9 S

   Answer:

3. 4 P N D 2 8 5 S K L B

   Answer:

4. E S 3 T 9 M X F 4 Y

   Answer:

5. T 2 4 L B S 9 N 5 P F

   Answer:

Arrange the letters in reverse alphabetical order followed by the numbers in ascending order.

6. J 4 N 2 6 3 P K Z D 7

   Answer:

7. 5 T L Y K X N 7 A M 3

   Answer:

8. D 9 2 K G H U 7 6 R

   Answer:

9. 8 A 9 7 T L S H 5 W J

   Answer:

10. G B M R 9 S K 4 3 2 W

    Answer:

# Agility of mind

Arrange the even numbers in ascending order followed by the letters in forward alphabetical order followed by the odd numbers in descending order.

11. Y 2 L 5 8 D 9 F G

    Answer: 28DFGLY95

12. S 7 5 2 4 K J T Z 6 3

    Answer: 246JKSTZ753

13. M 4 T N K F B 7 6 3 V 2 9

    Answer: 246BFKMNTV973

14. 7 6 Q P C H 8 4 3 T M A X

    Answer: 468ACHMPQTX73

15. D 8 K 3 J 2 X 9 T 5 B 4 U 7

    Answer: 248BDJKTUX9753

Arrange the odd numbers in ascending order followed by the letters in reverse alphabetical order followed by the even numbers in descending order.

16. J 6 N Q 5 7 D A F 8 K L

    Answer: 57QNLKJFDA86

17. 8 D 2 5 L H C J 7 4 6 9 3 T F

    Answer: 3579TLJHFDC8642

18. D 2 L 6 F N 3 M P Q J S 8 T 9

    Answer: 39TSQPNMLJFD862

19. 7 K 8 D F 9 T 6 J 2 L 5 S Q N

    Answer: 579TSQNLKJFD862

20. K F D C B 8 5 E N 7 T J 3 M 4

    Answer: 357TNMKJFEDCB84

## Answers to Test one

1. FALSE
2. TRUE
3. TRUE
4. TRUE
5. FALSE
6. TRUE
7. FALSE
8. FALSE (only dare, dear and read)
9. FALSE (666 – the first digit increases by 1 and the last digit decreases by 1)
10. TRUE
11. TRUE
12. TRUE
13. TRUE
14. FALSE (AbCdeFgHijKlM)
15. FALSE (the missing word should be DOT or COG, as CAT is being converted to DOG one letter at a time)
16. TRUE (72 + 28)
17. TRUE
18. TRUE
19. TRUE
20. FALSE

## Assessment

Score 1 point for each correct answer.

| | |
|---|---|
| 8–10 | Average |
| 11–13 | Good |
| 14–16 | Very good |
| 17–20 | Exceptional |

Transfer your score to the agility of mind overall assessment chart on page 42.

## Answers to Test two

1. admiral 2. orbital 3. tempest 4. consult 5. absence 6. episode 7. happier 8. tantrum 9. tourism 10. warmest 11. emerald 12. amiable 13. tarnish 14. earlier 15. glacier (or gracile) 16. calibre 17. replica 18. currant 19. tabloid 20. baronet 21. machine 22. satsuma 23. residue 24. drastic 25. festoon 26. curator 27. gumshoe 28. enforce 29. ceramic (or racemic) 30. emperor

## Assessment

Score 1 point for each correct answer.

| | |
|---|---|
| 12–17 | Average |
| 18–23 | Good |
| 24–27 | Very good |
| 28–30 | Exceptional |

Transfer your score to the agility of mind overall assessment chart on page 42.

## Answers to Test three

1. CODE
2. Tuesday, 15 April
3. 899 (23121 – 22222)
4. S (AbcDefgHijklMnopqrS)
5. 1 mile north
6. 32 (8 × 4)
7. Four-fifths of 995 (796). One-third of 2,385 = 795.
8. 35 minutes
9. 5364364563
10. 357SNKDCBA642
11. 11
12. ERMINE

13. 37 (+ 3, + 5, + 7, + 9, + 11)
14. £592
15. 26
16. TRIBAL
17. 50%. They are the percentage of vowels in each name.
18. 12
19. L
20. T and K

## Assessment

Score 1 point for each correct answer.

|       |           |
|-------|-----------|
| 8–11  | Average   |
| 12–15 | Good      |
| 16–17 | Very good |
| 18–20 | Exceptional |

Transfer your score to the agility of mind overall assessment chart on page 42.

## Answers to Test four

1. C 2. E 3. G 4. D 5. B 6. S 7. G 8. L 9. B 10. R

## Assessment

Score 1 point for each correct answer.

|      |             |
|------|-------------|
| 4–5  | Average     |
| 6–7  | Good        |
| 8    | Very good   |
| 9–10 | Exceptional |

Transfer your score to the agility of mind overall assessment chart on page 42.

## Answers to Test five

1. B K L N 6 8
2. A D F J N S T 5 8 9
3. B D K L N P S 2 4 5 8
4. E F M S T X Y 3 4 9
5. B F L N P S T 2 4 5 9
6. Z P N K J D 2 3 4 6 7
7. Y X T N M L K A 3 5 7
8. U R K H G D 2 6 7 9
9. W T S L J H A 5 7 8 9
10. W S R M K G B 2 3 4 9
11. 2 8 D F G L Y 9 5
12. 2 4 6 J K S T Z 7 5 3
13. 2 4 6 B F K M N T V 9 7 3
14. 4 6 8 A C H M P Q T X 7 3
15. 2 4 8 B D J K T U X 9 7 5 3
16. 5 7 Q N L K J F D A 8 6
17. 3 5 7 9 T L J H F D C 8 6 4 2
18. 3 9 T S Q P N M L J F D 8 6 2
19. 5 7 9 T S Q N L K J F D 8 6 2
20. 3 5 7 T N M K J F E D C B 8 4

## Assessment

Score 1 point for each correct answer.

| | |
|---|---|
| 8–11 | Average |
| 12–15 | Good |
| 16–17 | Very good |
| 18–20 | Exceptional |

Transfer your score to the agility of mind overall assessment chart on page 42.

## Agility of mind: overall assessment

| Test | Description | Score |
|---|---|---|
| One | Speed test – true or false | |
| Two | Verbal dexterity test | |
| Three | Eclectic agility of mind test | |
| Four | Find the letter test | |
| Five | Word and letter arrangement test | |
| Total score | | |

A total of 100 points is available in this chapter.

| | |
|---|---|
| 32–48 | Average |
| 49–78 | Good |
| 79–88 | Very good |
| 89–100 | Exceptional |

Divide your score by 2, round up to the nearest whole number and transfer the result to the overall brain quotient (BQ) rating chart on page 227.

# 3

# Tests of logical analysis

The *Concise Oxford English Dictionary* defines logic as *the science of reasoning, proof, thinking, or inference.*

In philosophy, logic (from the Greek *logos*, meaning 'word', 'speech' or 'reason') is a science that deals with the principles of valid reasoning and argument. A further definition of logical is *analytical* or *deductive*, and this definition can be applied to someone who is capable of reasoning, or using reason, in an orderly, well-argued fashion.

The tests and puzzles in this chapter do not require any specialized knowledge of mathematics or vocabulary in order to solve them, just the ability to think clearly and analytically and to follow a common-sense reasoning process.

## Test one: general test

You have 120 minutes in which to solve the 25 questions.

1.

| A | ? | D | E |
|---|---|---|---|
| C | D | ? | G |
| D | ? | G | H |
| F | G | I | J |

Which is the missing section?

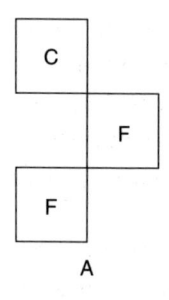

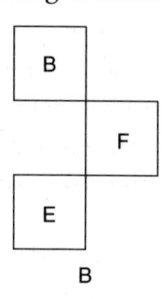

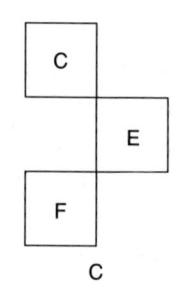

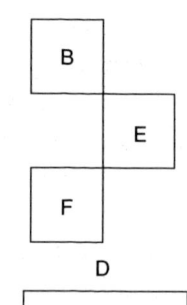

A.  C / F / F
B.  B / F / E
C.  C / E / F
D.  B / E / F

Answer:

2.

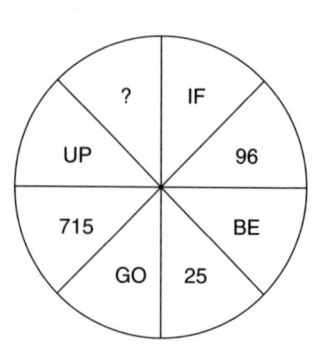

(Circle divided into 8 segments containing: ?, IF, 96, BE, 25, GO, 715, UP)

What should replace the question mark?

Answer:

3.

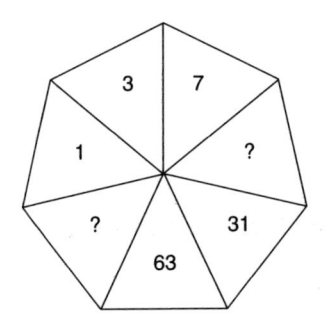

What numbers should replace the question marks?

Answer: ⬜

4.

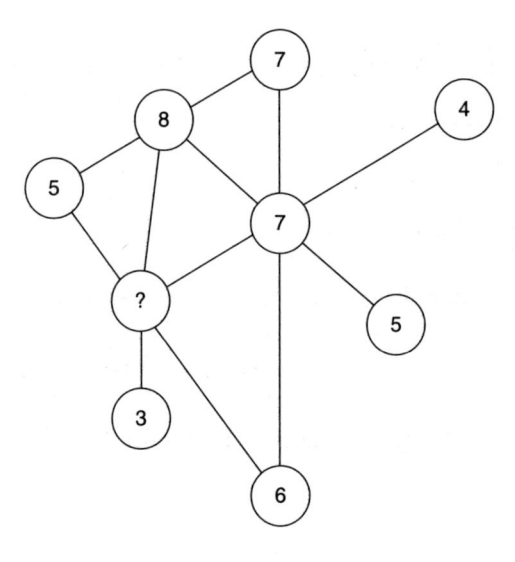

What number should replace the question mark?

Answer: ⬜

5. ICICLE
   EUREKA
   ?
   NORMAL
   LUXURY

   What word should replace the question mark?

   a. ABACUS
   b. MYSTIC
   c. FALCON
   d. ARISEN
   e. REASON

   Answer:

6. MARCH, MAY, AUGUST, OCTOBER, JANUARY, ?

   What comes next?

   Answer:

7. 364928, 109463, 94901, ?

   What number should replace the question mark?

   Answer:

8. Dickens, Kipling, Lehmann, Maugham, Golding

   Who comes next?

   a. Shelley
   b. Carroll
   c. Erasmus
   d. Tolkien
   e. Dodgson

   Answer:

## Tests of logical analysis

9.    MUSCLE        (SNORED)        ROTUND
      DILUTE        (? ? ? ? ? ?)   VALUES

What word is missing?

Answer: [          ]

10. 52, 97, 348, 26, 284, 37, 92, ?

What number should replace the question mark?

Answer: [          ]

11.

| 5 | 7 | 8 | 6 | 2 | 4 |
|---|---|---|---|---|---|
| 4 | 6 | 9 | 7 | 3 | 5 |

Study the logic by which the numbers in the top and bottom sets of six relate to each other and then fill in the missing numbers below:

| 6 | 7 | ? | 2 | 9 | 3 |
|---|---|---|---|---|---|
| 7 | 6 | 5 | ? | 8 | ? |

Answer: [          ]

12.

| 8 | 5 | 9 | 16 | 8 | 2 | ■ | 4 | 7 | 12 | 6 | 14 | 8 |
|---|---|---|---|---|---|---|---|---|---|---|---|---|
| 1 | 3 | 2 | 5 | 1 | 0 | ■ | ? | ? | ? | ? | ? | ? |

The top set of six numbers has a relationship to the set of six numbers below. The two sets of six boxes on the left have the same relationship as the two sets of six boxes on the right. Which set of numbers should, therefore, replace the question marks?

a. | 2 | 3 | 1 | 2 | 2 | 8 |

b. | 2 | 5 | 10 | 4 | 12 | 6 |

c. | 1 | 1 | 1 | 8 | 2 | 2 |

d. | 6 | 8 | 2 | 9 | 5 | 7 |

e. | 9 | 10 | 11 | 8 | 7 | 6 |

Answer: ☐

13. EMU
    WREN
    PITTA
    CUCKOO

   What comes next?

   a. BUZZARD
   b. PELICAN
   c. GOSHAWK
   d. QUETZAL
   e. WAXBILL

Answer: ☐

14. 7943162 is to 26347
    and 6825437 is to 73456
    therefore 6921584 is to ?

    Answer:

15. ode is to fondue as pig is to ?

    a. summer
    b. Barking
    c. Reading
    d. spring
    e. poke

    Answer:

16. monkey, hornet, wonder, loaned, longer, ?

    What comes next?

    a. cosine
    b. corner
    c. convoy
    d. throne
    e. confer

    Answer:

17. € ∂ ♪ € ∂ ♫ € ∂ ♪ € ∂ ♫ ?

    What figure comes next?

    a. €
    b. ∂
    c. €
    d. ∂

    Answer:

18. An electrical circuit wiring a set of four lights depends on a system of switches, A, B, C and D. Each switch when working has the following effect on the lights:

Switch A turns lights 1 and 2 on/off or off/on.
Switch B turns lights 2 and 4 on/off or off/on.
Switch C turns lights 1 and 3 on/off or off/on.
Switch D turns lights 3 and 4 on/off or off/on.

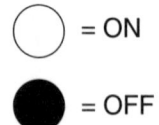

○ = ON

● = OFF

In the following diagram, switches C, B and D are thrown in turn, with the result that Set 1 is transformed into Set 2. One of the switches is not, therefore, working and has had no effect on the numbered lights. Identify which one of the switches is not working.

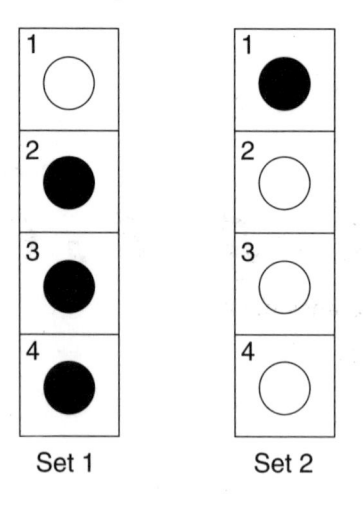

Answer:

19. An electrical circuit wiring a set of four lights depends on a system of switches A, B, C and D. Each switch when working has the following effect on the lights:

Switch A turns lights 1 and 2 on/off or off/on.
Switch B turns lights 2 and 4 on/off or off/on.
Switch C turns lights 1 and 3 on/off or off/on.
Switch D turns lights 3 and 4 on/off or off/on.

○ = ON

● = OFF

In the following diagram, switches D, B, C and A are thrown in turn, with the result that Set 1 is transformed into Set 2. One of the switches is not, therefore, working and has had no effect on the numbered lights. Identify which one of the switches is not working.

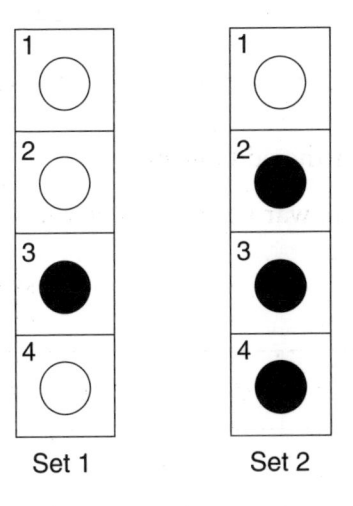

Set 1

Set 2

Answer:

20.

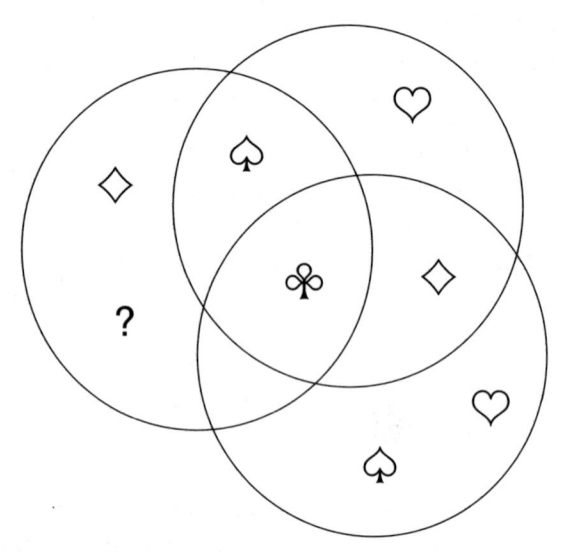

What should replace the question mark?

A ♠  B ♦  C 🔔  D ♡  E ☆

Answer:

21. Which word is the odd one out?

i. mad ii. ant iii. war iv. art v. rid vi. rim vii. saw

Answer:

22.

| S | A | C | U | N | E |
|---|---|---|---|---|---|
| N | E | T | O | R | ? |

What letter should replace the question mark?

Answer:

23. 1, 4, 19, 94, ?

    What number should replace the question mark?

    Answer:

24. open, toil, mope, unite, ?

    What comes next?

    a. lime
    b. orange
    c. fig
    d. apple

    Answer:

25. Two numbers are such that if the first receives 15 from the second they are in the ratio 2:1, but if the second receives 25 from the first they are in the ratio 1:3. What are the two numbers?

    Answer:

## Test two: progressive numerical matrix test

A matrix of numbers is displayed with one section missing. From the four choices presented you have to decide, by looking across each line and down each column, or at the matrix as a whole, just what pattern of numbers is occurring.

In each question there is sufficient information provided to establish what pattern or sequence is occurring looking at lines both across and down.

*Example:*

|   |   |   |
|---|---|---|
| 3 | 5 | 7 |
| 6 | 8 |   |
| 9 | 11 |  |

Which is the missing section?

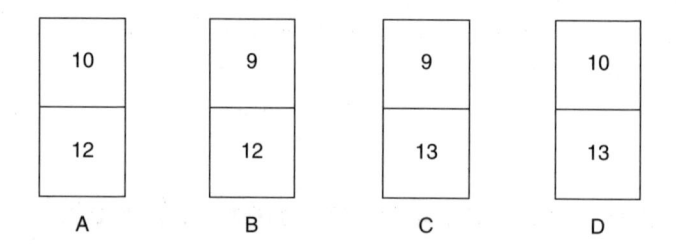

| A | B | C | D |
|---|---|---|---|
| 10 | 9 | 9 | 10 |
| 12 | 12 | 13 | 13 |

Answer: D

Explanation: Lines across progress + 2. Lines down progress + 3.

You have 60 minutes in which to solve the 15 questions.

Whilst the use of a calculator is not permitted in this test, it is recommended you have a supply of scrap paper in order to make notes and written calculations.

Tests of logical analysis  55

1.

|   |   |   |
|---|---|---|
| 5 | 3 | 1 |
| 7 | 5 |   |
| 9 |   | 5 |

Which is the missing section?

A: 4, 6
B: 3, 7
C: 4, 7
D: 3, 6

Answer:

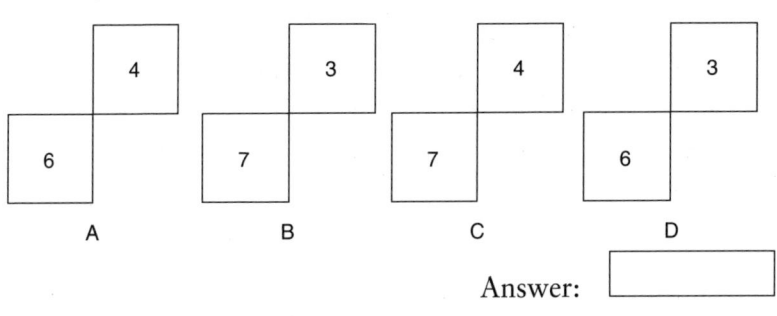

2.

| 2 | 4  | 6 |
| 5 | ?  | 9 |
| 8 | 10 | ? |

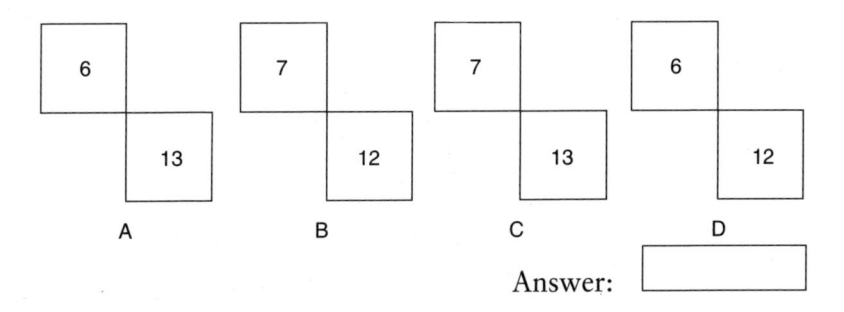

Which is the missing section?

A: 6, 13
B: 7, 12
C: 7, 13
D: 6, 12

Answer:

3.

| 1 | 2 | 4 |
|---|---|---|
| 4 | ? | 7 |
| ? | 9 | 11 |

Which is the missing section?

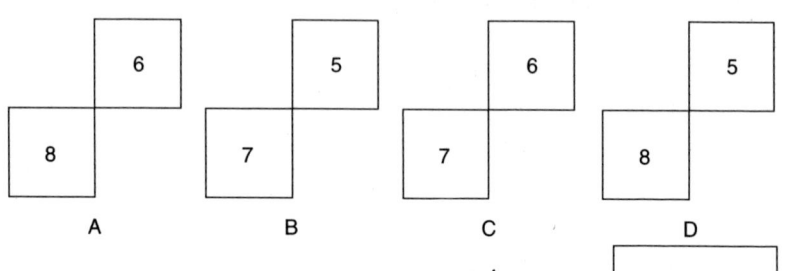

A: 6, 8
B: 5, 7
C: 6, 7
D: 5, 8

Answer:

4.

| 10 | ? | 8 |
|---|---|---|
| 15 | 11 | ? |
| 8 | ? | 6 |

Which is the missing section?

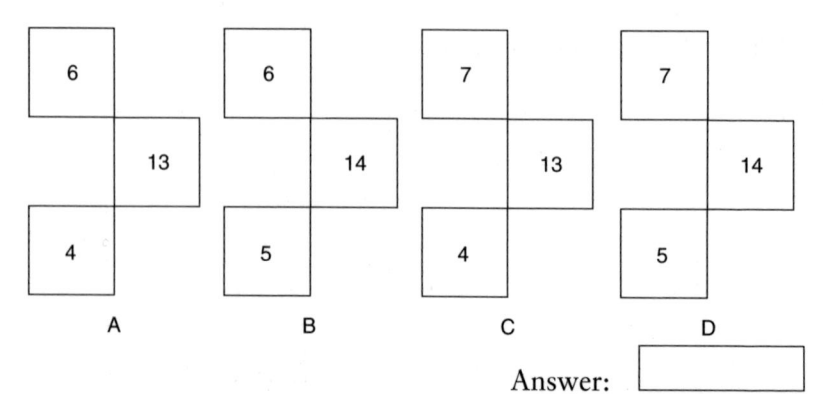

A: 6, 13, 4
B: 6, 14, 5
C: 7, 13, 4
D: 7, 14, 5

Answer:

5.

| 4 | 1 | 3 | 4 |
|---|---|---|---|
| 8 | ? | 7 | ? |
| 3 | 0 | ? | 3 |
| 6 | ? | 5 | 6 |

Which is the missing section?

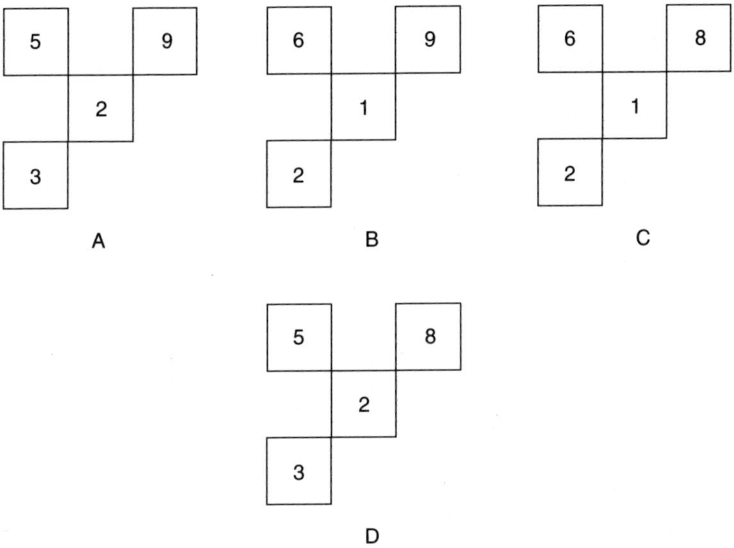

| 5 |   | 9 |
|---|---|---|
|   | 2 |   |
| 3 |   |   |

A

| 6 |   | 9 |
|---|---|---|
|   | 1 |   |
| 2 |   |   |

B

| 6 |   | 8 |
|---|---|---|
|   | 1 |   |
| 2 |   |   |

C

| 5 |   | 8 |
|---|---|---|
|   | 2 |   |
| 3 |   |   |

D

Answer:

58  Test and assess your brain quotient

6.

| 10 | 13 | ?  | 11 |
|----|----|----|----|
| 2  | 5  | ?  | 3  |
| 4  | ?  | 0  | ?  |
| 15 | ?  | 11 | 16 |

Which is the missing section?

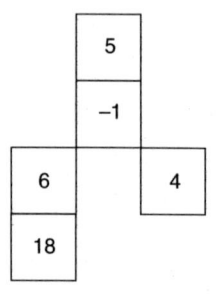

```
      5
     -1
  6     4
  18
     A
```

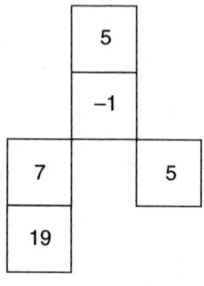

```
      5
     -1
  7     5
  19
     B
```

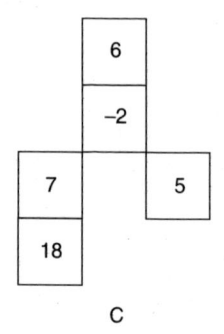

```
      6
     -2
  7     5
  18
     C
```

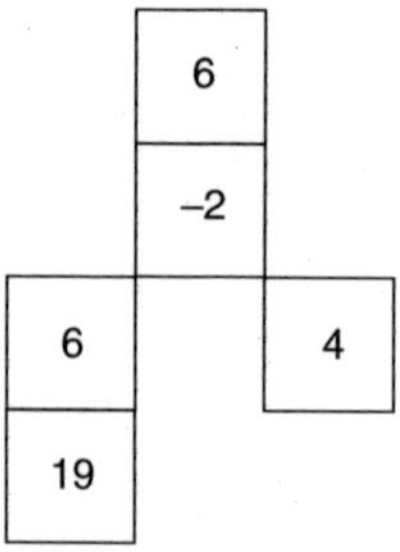

```
      6
     -2
  6     4
  19
     D
```

Answer: [    ]

7.

| 5 | 1 | ? | 10 |
|---|---|---|----|
| ? | ? | 3 | 5  |
| 12| 8 | ? | 17 |
| 4 | ? | 7 | 9  |

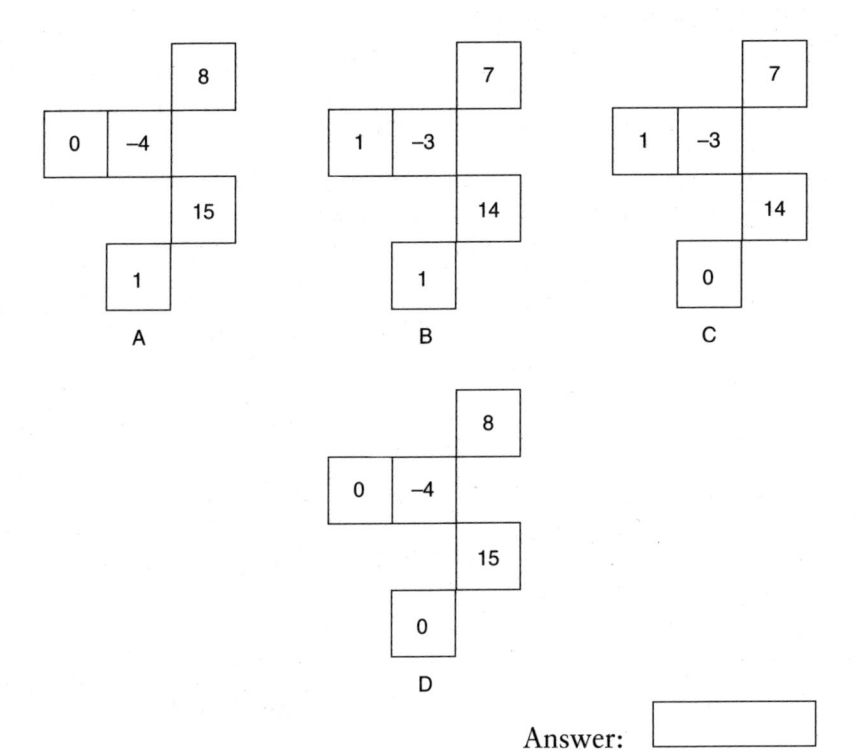

Which is the missing section?

A

B

C

D

Answer:

8.

| 9 | 5 | 12 | 15 |
|---|---|----|----|
| 16 | ? | ? | 22 |
| 19 | ? | ? | ? |
| ? | 6 | 13 | 16 |

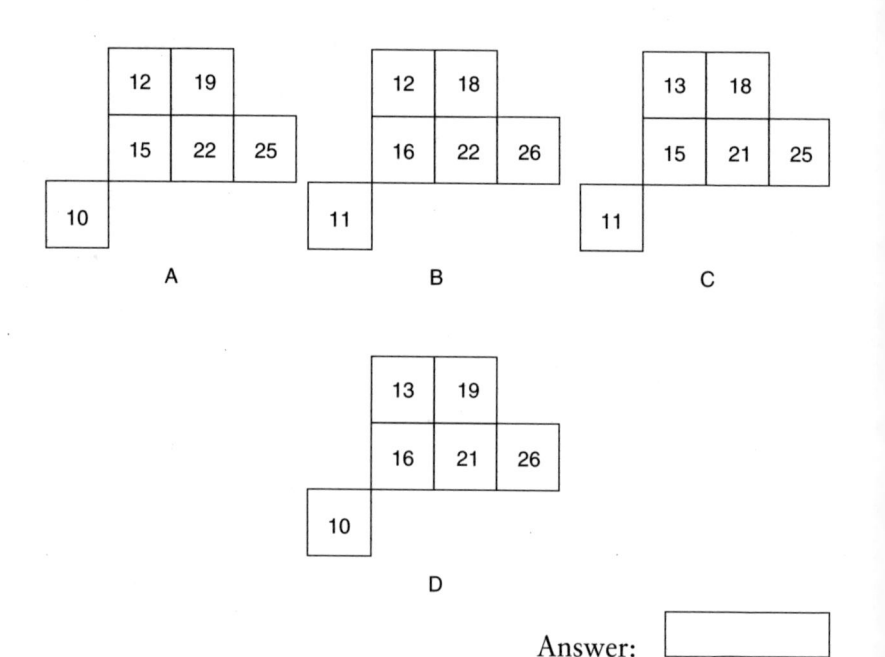

Which is the missing section?

```
     12 | 19
     15 | 22 | 25
10

     A
```

```
     12 | 18
     16 | 22 | 26
11

     B
```

```
     13 | 18
     15 | 21 | 25
11

     C
```

```
     13 | 19
     16 | 21 | 26
10

     D
```

Answer: ☐

Tests of logical analysis  61

9.

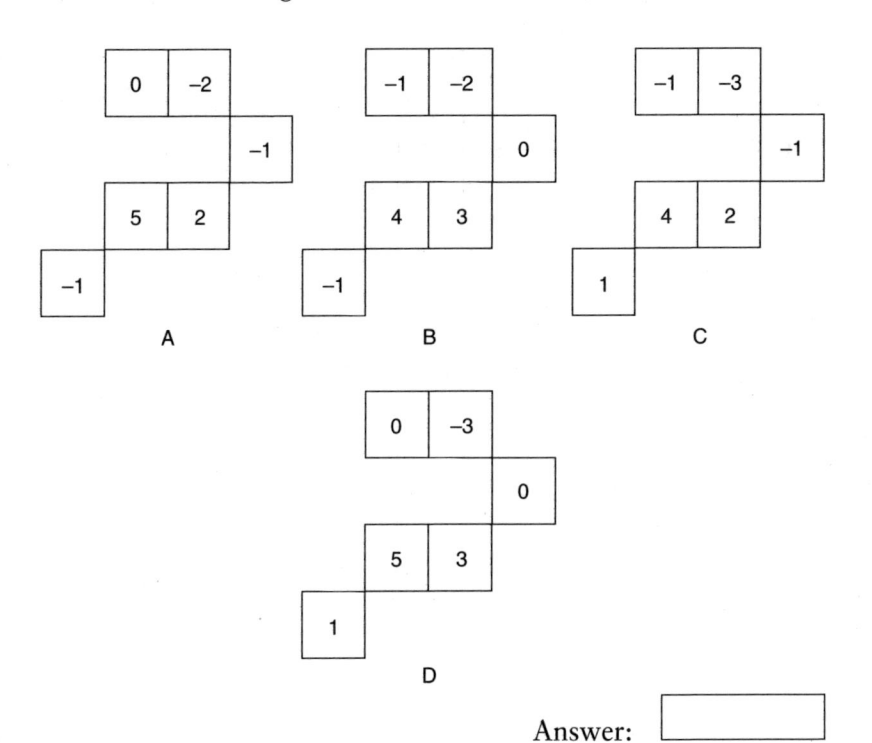

| 5 | ? | ? | 6 |
|---|---|---|---|
| −2 | −8 | −10 | ? |
| 10 | ? | ? | 11 |
| ? | −5 | −7 | 2 |

Which is the missing section?

```
   0  −2
          −1
   5   2
−1
       A
```

```
  −1  −2
          0
   4   3
−1
       B
```

```
  −1  −3
          −1
   4   2
 1
       C
```

```
   0  −3
          0
   5   3
 1
       D
```

Answer: ☐

62  Test and assess your brain quotient

10.

| 6 | ? | ? | −5 |
|---|---|---|---|
| 0 | ? | ? | −11 |
| 4 | ? | 2 | ? |
| −1 | 4 | −3 | ? |

Which is the missing section?

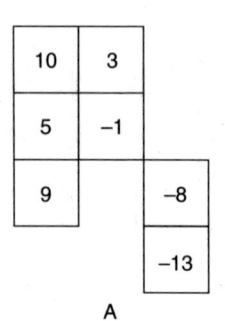

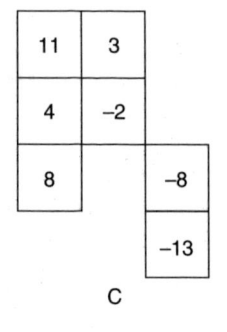

| 10 | 3 |    |
|----|----|----|
| 5  | −1 |    |
| 9  |    | −8 |
|    |    | −13 |

A

| 11 | 4 |    |
|----|----|----|
| 5  | −2 |    |
| 9  |    | −7 |
|    |    | −12 |

B

| 11 | 3 |    |
|----|----|----|
| 4  | −2 |    |
| 8  |    | −8 |
|    |    | −13 |

C

| 10 | 4 |    |
|----|----|----|
| 4  | −1 |    |
| 8  |    | −7 |
|    |    | −12 |

D

Answer:

Tests of logical analysis 63

11.

| 9 | ? | 20 | 5 |
|---|---|----|---|
| ? | 29 | 38 | ? |
| 12 | ? | ? | 8 |
| 29 | ? | 40 | 25 |

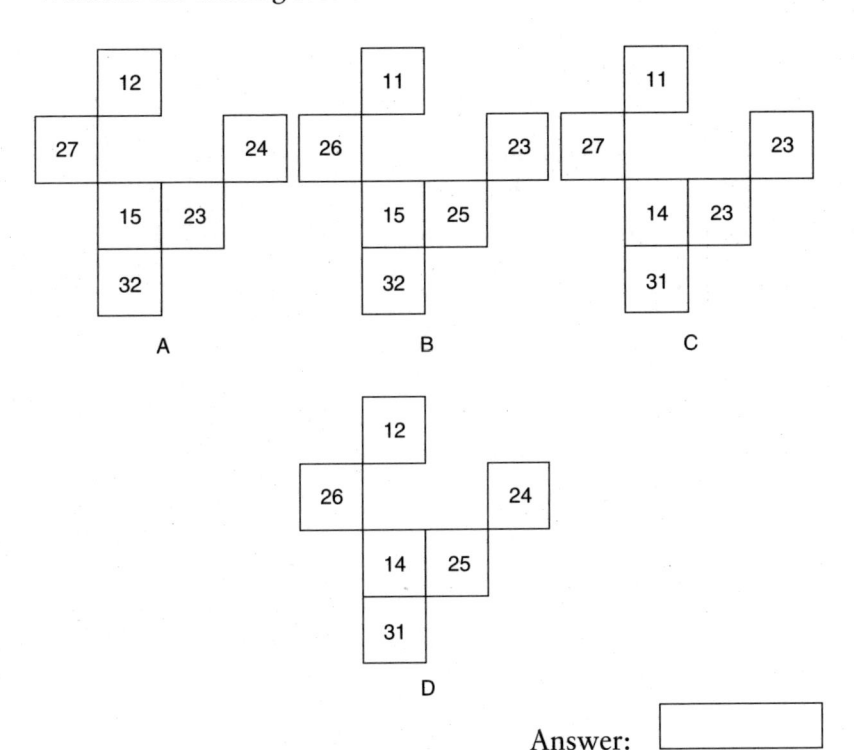

Which is the missing section?

A

```
      12
27        24
   15  23
   32
```

B

```
      11
26        23
   15  25
   32
```

C

```
      11
27        23
   14  23
   31
```

D

```
      12
26        24
   14  25
   31
```

Answer: [       ]

64  Test and assess your brain quotient

12.

| ? | 23 | ? | 18 | 32 |
|---|----|---|----|----|
| 2 | ? | 9 | 6 | ? |
| 19 | 28 | ? | 23 | ? |
| ? | 24 | ? | ? | 33 |
| 8 | ? | 15 | 12 | ? |

Which is the missing section?

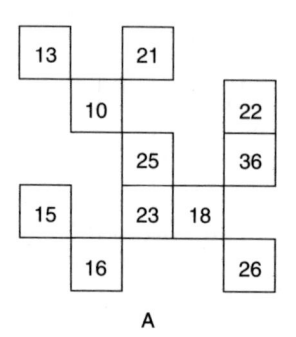

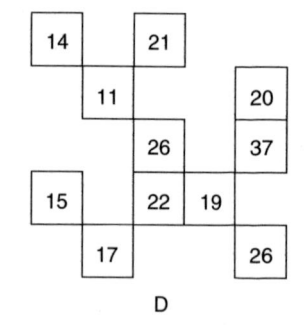

A

B

C

D

Answer:

Tests of logical analysis 65

13.

| 1 | 4 | −3 | −1 | ? |
|---|---|----|----|---|
| −3 | ? | ? | −5 | ? |
| 5 | ? | 1 | ? | ? |
| ? | ? | −5 | −3 | 16 |
| 14 | 17 | ? | ? | ? |

Which is the missing section?

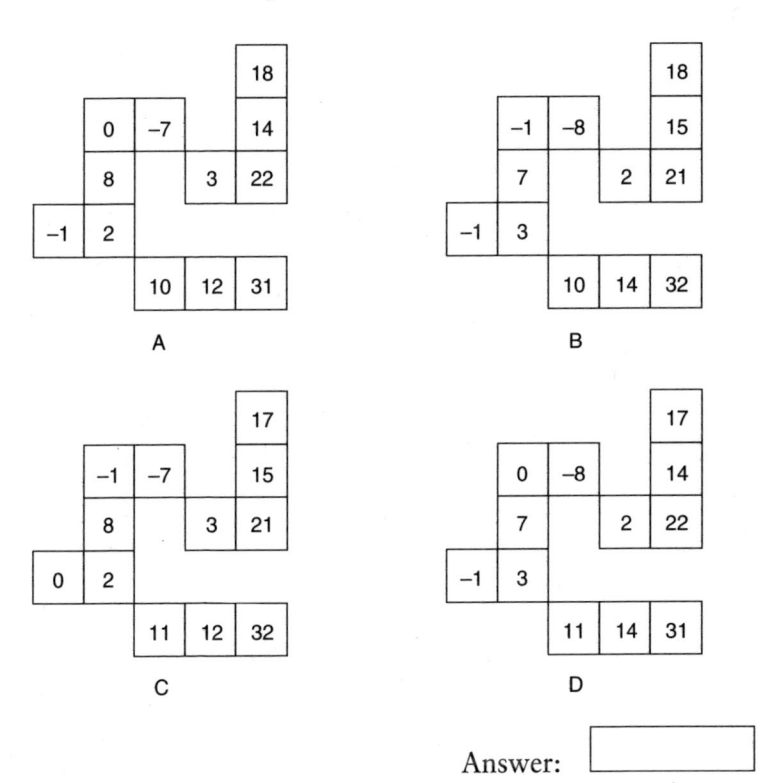

|   |   |   | 18 |   |
|---|---|---|----|---|
|   | 0 | −7 | 14 |   |
|   |   | 8 | 3 | 22 |
| −1 | 2 |   |   |   |
|   |   | 10 | 12 | 31 |

A

|   |   |   | 18 |   |
|---|---|---|----|---|
|   | −1 | −8 | 15 |   |
|   |   | 7 | 2 | 21 |
| −1 | 3 |   |   |   |
|   |   | 10 | 14 | 32 |

B

|   |   |   | 17 |   |
|---|---|---|----|---|
|   | −1 | −7 | 15 |   |
|   |   | 8 | 3 | 21 |
| 0 | 2 |   |   |   |
|   |   | 11 | 12 | 32 |

C

|   |   |   | 17 |   |
|---|---|---|----|---|
|   | 0 | −8 | 14 |   |
|   |   | 7 | 2 | 22 |
| −1 | 3 |   |   |   |
|   |   | 11 | 14 | 31 |

D

Answer: ☐

14.

| 7  | ?  | 43 | ?  | 21 |
|----|----|----|----|----|
| 25 | 40 | ?  | 25 | 39 |
| -6 | ?  | 30 | ?  | 8  |
| 1  | ?  | 37 | ?  | 15 |
| ?  | 42 | ?  | 27 | ?  |

Which is the missing section?

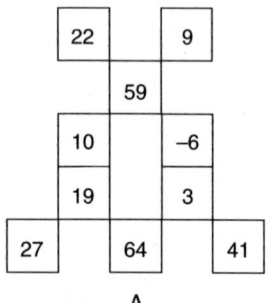

A

| 22 |    | 9  |
|    | 59 |    |
| 10 |    | -6 |
| 19 |    | 3  |
| 27 | 64 | 41 |

B

| 22 |    | 7  |
|    | 61 |    |
| 9  |    | -6 |
| 16 |    | 1  |
| 27 | 63 | 41 |

C

| 24 |    | 7  |
|    | 59 |    |
| 10 |    | -5 |
| 16 |    | 1  |
| 26 | 64 | 39 |

D

| 24 |    | 9  |
|    | 61 |    |
| 9  |    | -5 |
| 19 |    | 3  |
| 26 | 63 | 39 |

Answer:

15.

| 2 | 16 | 10 | 1 | 8 | −7 |
|---|----|----|---|---|----|
| 10 | ? | ? | ? | ? | 1 |
| 33 | ? | ? | ? | ? | 24 |
| 17 | ? | ? | ? | ? | 8 |
| 15 | ? | ? | ? | ? | 6 |
| 34 | 48 | 42 | 33 | 40 | 25 |

Which is the missing section?

| 24 | 17 | 8 | 16 |
|----|----|---|----|
| 46 | 41 | 30 | 38 |
| 32 | 25 | 15 | 24 |
| 29 | 22 | 13 | 20 |

A

| 23 | 18 | 9 | 15 |
|----|----|---|----|
| 47 | 39 | 30 | 38 |
| 31 | 24 | 15 | 23 |
| 27 | 22 | 14 | 21 |

B

| 23 | 17 | 8 | 15 |
|----|----|---|----|
| 46 | 39 | 32 | 39 |
| 32 | 24 | 16 | 24 |
| 27 | 23 | 13 | 20 |

C

| 24 | 18 | 9 | 16 |
|----|----|---|----|
| 47 | 41 | 32 | 39 |
| 31 | 25 | 16 | 23 |
| 29 | 23 | 14 | 21 |

D

Answer:

# Test three: symbolic complete the sequence test

In each of the 10 questions you have to work out which symbol, from the choice provided, will continue the sequence.

*Example:*

♣ ▶ & ♫ $ ♣ ▶ **&** ♪ $ ♣ ▶ &

Which symbol below continues the above sequence?

A. $
B. ♣
C. ♪
D. ▶

Answer: ☐ C

Explanation: The sequence consists of the figures: ♣ ▶ & ♪ $ repeated, and every fourth symbol is twice as large as the other symbols.

You have 30 minutes in which to complete the 10 questions.

1. ▲—▲▲—▲▲▲—▲▲▲▲—▲▲▲

   Which two symbols below continue the above sequence?

   A. —▲
   B. ▲▲
   C. ▲—

   Answer: ☐

2. ▶ * ♣ ♫ * ▲ ◀ — * $ • Ω ▶ * ♣ ♫ ▲ ◀ — * $ • Ω ▶ ♣ ♫ * ▲ ◀ — $ • Ω

   Which symbol below continues the above sequence?

   A. *

   B. ♫

   C. ▶

   D. ◀

   Answer: ☐

3. ☼ & π ☺ $ ♪ ╬ ♪ $ ☺ π &

   Which symbol below completes the above sequence?

   A. π

   B. $

   C. ☼

   D. ╬

   Answer: ☐

4. ◙ ♠ ♫ Ω ▤ ◀ ◊ ∩ ≠ ∏ ◙ ♠ ♫ Ω ▤ ◀ ◊ ∩ ≠ ∏ ? ? ♫ Ω ▤ ◀ ◊ ∩ ≠ ∏

   Which two symbols below should replace the question marks in the above sequence?

   A. ◀ ▤

   B. ◙ ♠

   C. Ω ▤

   D. ♠ ◙

   Answer: ☐

5. ∦ π ᴨ ⊥ ⊥ ╪ ╫ ╟ ∦ π ᴨ ⊥ ⊥ ╪ ╫ ╟ ∦ π ᴨ ⊥ ⊥ ╪ ╫

Which symbol below continues the above sequence?

A. ∦
B. π
C. ⊥
D. ╟

Answer: [ ]

6. •■♠△↕¶¥# •■♠△↕¶¥# •■♠△↕¶¥#

Which two symbols below continue the above sequence?

A. △■
B. •■
C. •■
D. ■•

Answer: [ ]

7. ∘○•○∘●∘○•○∘●∘○•○∘●∘○•○

Which three symbols below continue the above sequence?

A. ∘○•
B. ∘●∘
C. ○∘•
D. ∘•○

Answer: [ ]

## Tests of logical analysis 71

8. ♣♪♥♠←♣♪♥♠↑♣♪♥♠→♣♪♥♠

   Which two symbols below continue the above sequence?

   A. ←♣

   B. ↑♦

   C. ↓♣

   D. ♣→

   Answer:

9. ▶■■■■■▲■■■■◀■■■▼■■▶■▶■■■■???■■■◀■■■▼■■▶■

   Which three symbols below should replace the question marks?

   A. ▲■■

   B. ■▲■

   C. ■▼■

   D. ■■▲

   Answer:

10. ↑♦♠↓?♥●☺◉■◀♀↑♦♠↓←♥●☺◉■◀♀

    Which symbol below should replace the question mark?

    A. →

    B. ↓

    C. ←

    D. ↑

    Answer:

## Answers to Test one

1. B. Lines across progress in the pattern ABcDE. Lines down progress in the pattern AbCDeF.
2. 2116. Looking clockwise each number represents the position of the letters in the alphabet of the preceding word. So UP = 2116, the 21st and 16th letters of the alphabet.
3. 15 and 127. Start at 1 and spiral clockwise adding 2, 4, 8, 16, 32, 64.
4. 9. Each connected straight line of three numbers totals 20.
5. d. ARISEN. Each word starts with the same letter as the last letter of the previous word.
6. MARCH. Miss one month and then two months alternately.
7. 1949. Add the last two digits and reverse the remaining digits each time.
8. e. Dodgson. Each name commences with the fourth letter of the previous name.
9. LEAVES

   M U S C L E    (S N O R E D)    R O T U N D
      1     5      1 2 3 4 5 6      4 3     2 6
   D I L U T E    (L E A V E S)    V A L U E S

10. 5. The sequence is then palindromic (it reads the same backwards and forwards).
11. 

| 6 | 7 | 4 | 2 | 9 | 3 |
|---|---|---|---|---|---|
| 7 | 6 | 5 | 3 | 8 | 2 |

   Looking from top to bottom, add 1 to even numbers and subtract 1 from odd numbers.
12. c. Add pairs of numbers: 4 + 7 = 11, 12 + 6 = 18 and 14 + 8 = 22.
13. d. QUETZAL. Each word commences with the letter two places in the alphabet after the last letter of the previous

word, ie EMU (v) WREN (o) PITTA (b) CUCKOO (p) QUETZAL.
14. 48526. Reverse the previous number and discard the lowest and highest digits.
15. d. spring: ode is the second, fourth and sixth letters of fondue as pig is the second, fourth and sixth letters of spring.
16. b. corner. The letters 'o', 'n' and 'e' occupy the second, third and fifth, and second, fourth and fifth positions in the words alternately.
17. c. The sequence consists of three repeated symbols and every second symbol is twice as large as the rest.
18. Switch D is faulty.
19. Switch B is faulty.
20. D: so that each circle contains one each of the four suits, clubs, spades, hearts and diamonds.
21. iv. art. Combine the words numbered i and v, ii and vi, iii and vii to produce Madrid, Antrim, Warsaw.
22. D. Alternate letters top to bottom and then bottom to top spell out SECOND NATURE.
23. 469
    × 5 − 1
24. a. lime. Take out all the vowels to leave p n t l m, repeated in the same order.
25. 49 and 47

## Assessment

Score 1 point for each correct answer.

| | |
|---|---|
| 10–13 | Average |
| 14–17 | Good |
| 18–22 | Very good |
| 23–25 | Exceptional |

Transfer your score to the tests of logical analysis overall assessment chart on page 76.

## Answers to Test two

1. B. Looking across lines progress − 2. Looking down lines progress + 2.
2. B. Looking across lines progress + 2. Looking down lines progress + 3.
3. D. Looking across lines progress + 1, + 2. Looking down lines progress + 3, + 4.
4. A. Looking across lines progress − 4, + 2. Looking down lines progress + 5, − 7.
5. D. Looking across lines progress − 3, + 2, + 1. Looking down lines progress + 4, − 5, + 3.
6. C. Looking across lines progress + 3, − 7, + 5. Looking down lines progress − 8, + 2, + 11.
7. D. Looking across lines progress − 4, + 7, + 2. Looking down lines progress − 5, + 12, − 8.
8. A. Looking across lines progress − 4, + 7, + 3. Looking down lines progress + 7, + 3, − 9.
9. C. Looking across lines progress − 6, − 2, + 9. Looking down lines progress − 7, + 12, − 9.
10. B. Looking across lines progress + 5, − 7, − 9. Looking down lines progress − 6, + 4, − 5.
11. C. Looking across lines progress + 2, + 9, − 15. Looking down lines progress + 18, − 15, + 17.
12. D. Looking across lines progress + 9, − 2, − 3, + 14. Looking down lines progress − 12, + 17, − 4, − 7.
13. A. Looking across lines progress + 3, − 7, + 2, + 19. Looking down lines progress − 4, + 8, − 6, + 15.
14. B. Looking across lines progress + 15, + 21, − 36, + 14. Looking down lines progress + 18, − 31, + 7, + 26.
15. D. Looking across lines progress + 14, − 6, − 9, + 7, − 15. Looking down lines progress + 8, + 23, − 16, − 2, + 19.

## Assessment

Score 1 point for each correct answer.

| | |
|---|---|
| 6–7 | Average |
| 8–10 | Good |
| 11–12 | Very good |
| 13–15 | Exceptional |

Transfer your score to the tests of logical analysis overall assessment chart on page 76.

## Answers to Test three

1. B. The sequence progresses one triangle, line, two triangles, line, three triangles, line, etc.
2. C. The sequence consists of the repeated symbols ▶ ♣ ♪ ▲ ◀ — $ • Ω. The star is inserted after one symbol, then two symbols, then three symbols, etc.
3. C: so that the sequence is palindromic, ie it reads the same both backwards and forwards.
4. B. The sequence consists of the repeated symbols ◙ ♠ ♪ Ω ▓ ◀ △ ∩ ≠ ∏
5. D. The sequence consists of the repeated symbols ∦ ╥ ╦ ⊥ ⊥ ╪ ╫ ╟
6. B. The sequence consists of the repeated symbols • ■ ♠ Δ ↕ ¶ ¥ # and every third symbol is twice as large as the rest.
7. B. Every third dot is black and every alternate dot is twice as large.
8. C. The sequence consists of the repeated symbols ♣ ♪ ♥ ♠. Each set is followed by an arrow that points west, north, east and south in turn.
9. B. The sequence consists of the repeated symbols ▶■■■■■ ▲■■■■◀■■■▼■■▶■
10. C. The sequence consists of the repeated symbols: ↑ ♦ ♠ ↓ ← ♥ • ☺ ◙ ■ ◀ ♀

## Assessment

Score 1 point for each correct answer.

| | |
|---|---|
| 4–5 | Average |
| 6–7 | Good |
| 8 | Very good |
| 9–10 | Exceptional |

Transfer your score to the tests of logical analysis overall assessment chart below.

# Tests of logical analysis: overall assessment

| Test | Description | Score |
|---|---|---|
| One | General test | |
| Two | Progressive numerical matrix test | |
| Three | Symbolic complete the sequence test | |
| Total score | | |

A total of 50 points is available in this chapter.

| | |
|---|---|
| 16–24 | Average |
| 25–34 | Good |
| 35–44 | Very good |
| 45–50 | Exceptional |

Transfer your score to the overall brain quotient (BQ) rating chart on page 227.

# 4

# *Tests of numerical aptitude*

Numerical tests generally explore your ability to reason and to perform basic arithmetic functions. Sometimes flexibility of thought and lateral thinking processes are also necessary in order to solve the problems that are presented.

It is accepted that numerical (mathematical) intelligence is a strong indicator of general intelligence, as many everyday tasks require arithmetical operations or thought processes, even though numbers may not be involved.

Individual numerical tests include mental arithmetic, number sequences and logical reasoning, all designed to test a person's aptitude and ability at mathematical calculation, identifying number patterns and the ability to reason with numbers.

## Test one: sequences

In a numerical sequence test it is necessary to identify a pattern that is occurring in the sequence. The numbers in the sequence may be progressing, or they may be decreasing, and in some cases they may be both progressing and decreasing within the sequence. It is up to you to determine how this is occurring and either to continue the sequence or to provide a missing number within the sequence.

For example, in the following sequence:

1, 9, 17, 25, 33, ?

the missing number is 41, as the numbers in the sequence are increasing by 8 each time.

However, in the more complex sequence:

100, 99, 97, 96, 94, 93, ?

the missing number is 91, as the numbers in the sequence are decreasing by 1 and then 2 alternately.

You have 75 minutes in which to solve the 30 questions. The use of a calculator is not allowed in this test.

1. 13, 17, 21, ?, 29, 33

    Answer:

2. 7, 11, 16, 22, 29, ?

    Answer:

3. 56, 48, 37, 23, ?

    Answer:

4. 64, 76, ?, 103, 118, 134

    Answer:

5. 100, 93, 84, 73, ?, 45

    Answer:

6. 13, 26, 39, ?, 65, 78

    Answer:

7. 1, 1, 4, 2, 9, 4, 16, 7, 25, ?, ?

   Answer:

8. 100, 50, 96, 53, 88, 59, 72, 71, ?, ?

   Answer:

9. 1, 2, 8, 16, 64, ?

   Answer:

10. 7.5, 8.75, 10, 11.25, ?

    Answer:

11. 382, 13, 169, 16, 256, 13, ?, ?

    Answer:

12. 1,000, 875, 725, ?, 350, 125

    Answer:

13. 50, 35, 15, ?, −40

    Answer:

14. 36, 72, ?, 144, 180

    Answer:

15. 1, 15, 3, 13, 6, 10, 10, 6, 15, 1, ?, ?

    Answer:

16. 64, 10, 54, ?, ?, 9, 36, 9, 27

    Answer:

17. 17.5, 15.25, ?, 10.75, 8.5

    Answer:

18. 3½, 5¾, ?, 10¼, 12½, 14¾

Answer:

19. 19, 38, 114, 228, ?, 1,368

Answer:

20. 60, ?, 52.5, 48.75, 45, 41.25, 37.5

Answer:

21. 48, 97, 195, 391, ?

Answer:

22. 98, 91, 82, 75, 66, ?, 50

Answer:

*Questions 23–30:*
In each of the following questions, in the two numerical sequences given, one number that appears in the top sequence should appear in the bottom sequence and vice versa. Which two numbers should be changed round in each question?

23. 12, 24, 40, 54, 84, 112
    10, 18, 28, 40, 60, 70

Answer:

24. 18, 21, 29, 45, 66, 93
    27, 30, 33, 41, 57, 89

Answer:

25. 100, 86, 68, 50, 20, –10
    110, 93, 73, 46, 24, –5

Answer:

26. 12, 34, 61, 93, 130, 172, 212, 271
    8, 27, 52, 83, 120, 163, 219, 267

    Answer:

27. 6, 15, 22, 31, 38, 47, 53
    14, 21, 30, 37, 46, 54, 62

    Answer:

28. 49, 45, 40, 36, 31, 29, 22
    51, 46, 40, 35, 27, 24, 18

    Answer:

29. 2, 5, 14, 41, 127, 365, 1,094
    3, 7, 15, 31, 63, 122, 255

    Answer:

30. 2, 3, 5, 8, 11, 21, 34
    3, 4, 7, 13, 18, 29, 47

## Test two: mental arithmetic test

The use of a calculator is not allowed in this test, and only the answer must be committed to paper, as all the calculations must be worked out in the head. You have 45 minutes in which to solve the 30 questions.

1. What is 9 multiplied by 5?

   Answer:

2. What is 72 divided by 3?

   Answer:

3. What is 7 multiplied by 8?

   Answer:

4. What is 50% of 196?

   Answer: ____

5. What is 12 multiplied by 7?

   Answer: ____

6. What is 70% of 110?

   Answer: ____

7. Multiply 15 by 11.

   Answer: ____

8. Multiply 12 by 9 and divide by 4.

   Answer: ____

9. What is ¾ of 228?

   Answer: ____

10. What is 15 + 18 + 12 + 36?

    Answer: ____

11. What is (36 × 3) divided by (3 × 4)?

    Answer: ____

12. What is (7 × 6) + (8 × 9)?

    Answer: ____

13. Multiply 3 × 4 × 6.

    Answer: ____

14. Multiply 16 by 5 and subtract (6 × 4).

    Answer: ____

15. What is 90% of 120?

    Answer: _____

16. What is five-sixths of 192?

    Answer: _____

17. Add 597 to 136.

    Answer: _____

18. Subtract 829 from 1,752.

    Answer: _____

19. Multiply 72 by 15.

    Answer: _____

20. What is 62 + 96 + 47?

    Answer: _____

21. What is 2.96 plus 17.58?

    Answer: _____

22. What is 60% of 1,950?

    Answer: _____

23. What is 200 divided by 16?

    Answer: _____

24. What is three-sixteenths expressed as a decimal?

    Answer: _____

25. Multiply 139 by 9.

    Answer: _____

26. What is three-fifths of 1,690?

Answer: ☐

27. What is three-ninths of 1,269?

Answer: ☐

28. What is 55% of 270?

Answer: ☐

29. Deduct two-thirds of 69 from 100.

Answer: ☐

30. Add 42,967 to 8,312.

Answer: ☐

## Test three: complete the equation test

This test consists of 15 questions in which you are given an incomplete equation and must find the missing part of the equation from the choices available. The time limit allowed for completing this test is 60 minutes. The use of a calculator is not permitted in this test; however, it is recommended you have some scrap paper available to make notes.

*Questions 1–5:*
Work out what number should replace the question mark to complete the equation correctly.

1. | 5 | ? | 6 | + | 3 | 9 | = | 6 | 2 | 5 |

Answer: ☐

2. | 2 | 9 | ? | ÷ | 9 | 7 | = | 3 |

Answer: [ ]

3. | 6 | ? | ÷ | 4 | = | 1 | 5 | 3 | ÷ | 9 |

Answer: [ ]

4. | 4 | 5 | . | 8 | × | 7 | = | 3 | 2 | ? | . | 6 |

Answer: [ ]

5. | 3 | . | ? | 5 | × | 6 | = | 2 | 2 | . | 5 |

Answer: [ ]

*Questions 6–15:*
Complete the equation by correctly identifying the missing part of the calculation from the list of options provided.

6. $\dfrac{?}{4+5} = \dfrac{84}{12}$
   a. $7 \times 8$
   b. $45 + 18$
   c. $110 - 49$
   d. $17 \times 4$
   e. $19 + 7^2$

Answer: [ ]

7. $\dfrac{(9 \times 8) \div 6}{?} = 0.375 + 0.125$

   a. $5^2$
   b. $4^2 + 9$
   c. $5^3 - 102$
   d. $12.5\% \times 184$
   e. $3^3 - 3$

   Answer: ☐

8. $0.5 (16 \times 12) + (?) = 11^2 + (3^2 + 18)$

   a. $(68 \div 2) + 14$
   b. $(17 \times 3)$
   c. $(132 - 90)$
   d. $(13 \times 4)$
   e. $(60\% \times 106)$

   Answer: ☐

9. $\dfrac{(37 \times 3) + 13^2}{4^3 + 4^2} = ?$

   a. $\dfrac{17.5}{5}$

   b. $1.6 + 2.9$

   c. $\dfrac{3}{8} \times 6$

   d. $8 + 3/5$

   e. $\dfrac{14.4}{6}$

   Answer: ☐

10. $\sqrt{(?)} + 2 = \dfrac{3{,}987}{443}$

 a. (18.5 +17.5)

 b. $\dfrac{5^2}{2^3}$

 c. (0.375 × 20)

 d. $\dfrac{8.4 \times 15}{2}$

 e. (9.8 × 5)

Answer:

11. $\dfrac{(63 \times 4) + 3}{85 \div \sqrt{25}} = \dfrac{?}{7.5}$

 a. 120
 b. 108.75
 c. 37 × 3
 d. 112.5
 e. 105

Answer:

12. $63 + (48 \times ?) = 9^2 + (20\% \times 90)$

    a. 4/5
    b. 60%
    c. 0.85
    d. $2^2$
    e. 0.75

    Answer:

13. $\dfrac{3}{12} \div ? = 1.125$

    a. 1/3
    b. 5/8
    c. 2/9
    d. 45%
    e. 0.46

    Answer:

14. $159 - (? - 57) = \dfrac{366}{122} - \dfrac{225}{75}$

    a. $(9 \times 23)$
    b. $6^3$
    c. $4^4$
    d. $(500 - 274)$
    e. 218

    Answer:

15. $\dfrac{1{,}350}{225} = \dfrac{?}{0.75} + \dfrac{518}{259}$

   a. 4
   b. 4.5
   c. 6
   d. 3
   e. 7.5

   Answer: ☐

## Test four: general numerical test

You have 120 minutes in which to complete the 25 questions. The use of a calculator is permitted in this test.

1. Looking at straight rows of numbers horizontally, vertically and diagonally, what number is three places away from itself plus 2, two places away from itself multiplied by 3 and two places away from itself less 3?

| 17 | 11 | 28 | 15 | 9 |
|---|---|---|---|---|
| 24 | 4 | 8 | 12 | 6 |
| 18 | 22 | 2 | 13 | 20 |
| 13 | 7 | 16 | 21 | 33 |
| 5 | 1 | 10 | 66 | 3 |

Answer: ☐

2. Insert the numbers listed into the circles so that – for any particular circle – the sum of the numbers in the circles connected to it equals the value corresponding to that circled number in the list.

   *For example:*

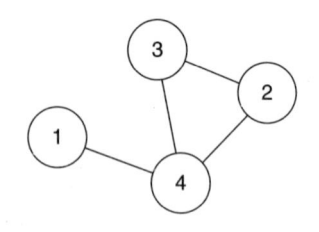

   1 = 4
   2 = 7 (3 + 4)
   3 = 6 (4 + 2)
   4 = 6 (3 + 2 + 1)

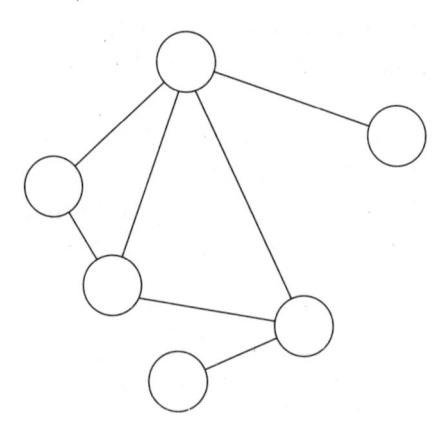

   1 = 8
   2 = 5
   3 = 10
   4 = 14
   5 = 10
   6 = 4

   Answer:

3. What number should replace the question mark?

   3874 (112)     2869 (97)     8627 (?)

   Answer: [ ]

4. Barry is one and a quarter times as old as Carrie, who is one and a quarter times as old as Harry. Their total ages are 122. How old are Harry, Carrie and Barry?

   Answer: [ ]

5. If A = 3, B = 7, C = 8 and D = 9, calculate:

   $$\frac{(A \times B) + (D \times C)}{\sqrt[3]{(A \times D)}}$$

   Answer: [ ]

6. How many minutes is it before noon if 16 minutes ago it was three times as many minutes past 8 am?

   Answer: [ ]

7.

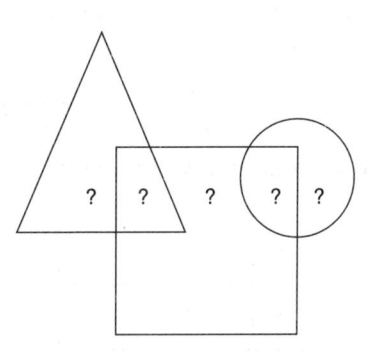

   The question marks represent five consecutive odd numbers. When added together the numbers in the triangle = 52, the numbers in the square = 87. What are the five numbers?

   Answer: [ ]

8. Between 11 am and 12 noon the office received 99 e-mails, which was 65% more than the number of e-mails it received between 10 am and 11 am. How many e-mails were received between 10 am and 11 am?

Answer:

9. During the first week of a sale a coat originally costing £86 was reduced by 10%. At the beginning of the second week it was marked down by a further 15%. What was the final sale price?

Answer:

10. I travel to work by train and bus. If my train journey takes 49 minutes and my bus journey takes 17 minutes longer, what is my total travelling time in hours and minutes?

Answer:

11. 7 6 5 3 1 9 7 2 5 6 3 8 2 1

Delete all the numbers that appear more than once in the above list and multiply the remaining numbers together. What is the total?

Answer:

12. What number should replace the question mark?

| 3 | 9  | 7  | 5 |
|---|----|----|---|
| 8 | 7  | 11 | 4 |
| 9 | 5  | 6  | 8 |
| 2 | 11 | 12 | ? |

Answer:

13. I completed a journey by rail, bus and taxi. If the train fare cost £89.65, the taxi fare cost £68.27 less than the train fare, and the bus fare cost £19.50 less than the taxi fare, how much did the total journey cost me?

    Answer:

14. What number should replace the question mark?

    3629 (7)        4967 (18)        6892 (?)

    Answer:

15. What number should replace the question mark?

    3826 : 78
    5213 : 24
    8564 : 76
    6325 : ?

    Answer:

16. 9386 : 2748 : 1432
    8479 : 3263 : 618

    Which numbers below have the same relationship to each other as the two sets of numbers above?

    a. 9265 : 5410 : 20
    b. 6874 : 4828 : 864
    c. 4853 : 3215 : 65
    d. 7429 : 2794 : 44
    e. 3946 : 2742 : 148

    Answer:

17. What is the decimal value of:

    $$\frac{3}{9} \div \frac{5}{6}$$

    Answer:

18. In a right-angled triangle, what is the length of the shortest side if the length of the hypotenuse is 78 cm and the length of the second-longest side is 72 cm?

    Answer:

19. 5, 15, 26, 38, 51, ?

    What number continues the sequence?

    Answer:

20. Each set of nine numbers relates to the other in a certain way. Work out the logic behind the numbers in the left-hand box in order to determine which number is missing from the right-hand box.

    | 2 | 5 | 8 | 3 | 5 | 9 |
    |---|---|---|---|---|---|
    | 8 | 9 | 8 | 2 | ? | 2 |
    | 7 | 4 | 1 | 9 | 7 | 6 |

    Answer:

21. What is the value of −45 − −32?

    Answer:

22. In a game of eight players lasting for 75 minutes, four reserves alternate equally with each player. For how long is each player, including the reserves, on the field of play?

    Answer:

23. A company produces red, green and blue widgets in the ratio 2:7:4. If a week's production totals 7,774 widgets, how many green widgets are produced?

    Answer:

24. What is the value of −16 + −5 ?

    Answer:

25. In a consignment of tomatoes, 339 had mould on them, which was 15 per cent of the total consignment. How many tomatoes were in the consignment?

    Answer:

## Answers to Test one

1. 25. Add 4 each time.
2. 37. Add 4, 5, 6, 7, 8.
3. 6. Subtract 8, 11, 14, 17.
4. 89. Add 12, 13, 14, 15, 16.
5. 60. Subtract 7, 9, 11, 13, 15.
6. 52. Add 13 each time.
7. 11, 36. There are two alternate sequences. From the first 1 add 3, 5, 7, 9. From the second 1 add 1, 2, 3, 4.
8. 40, 95. There are two alternate sequences. From 100 subtract 4, 8, 16, 32. From 50 add 3, 6, 12, 24.
9. 128
   × 2, × 4, × 2, × 4, etc
10. 12.5. Add 1.25 each time.
11. 169, 16. Add the digits and then square the result, ie 13 × 13 = 169 and 1 + 6 + 9 = 16.
12. 550. Subtract 125, 150, 175, 200, 225.
13. −10. Subtract 15, 20, 25, 30.
14. 108. Add 36 each time.
15. 21, −5. There are two alternate sequences. From 1 add 2, 3, 4, 5, 6. From 15 subtract 2, 3, 4, 5, 6.
16. 9, 45. Add the digits and then deduct.
    6 + 4 = 10, 64 − 10 = 54, 5 + 4 = 9, 54 − 9 = 45
17. 13. Subtract 2.25 each time.
18. 8. Subtract 2¼ each time.
19. 684
    × 2, × 3 repeated
20. 56.25. Subtract 3.75 each time.
21. 783
    × 2 + 1 each time
22. 59
    − 7, − 9, etc
23. 54 and 60. Top sequence: add 12, 16, 20, 24, 28. Bottom sequence: add 8, 10, 12, 14, 16.

24. 29 and 30. Top sequence: add 3, 9, 15, 21, 27. Bottom sequence: add 2, 4, 8, 16, 32.
25. 50 and 46. Top sequence: subtract 14, 18, 22, 26, 30. Bottom sequence: subtract 17, 20, 23, 26, 29.
26. 212 and 219. Top sequence: add 22, 27, 32, 37, 42, 47, 52. Bottom sequence: add 19, 25, 31, 37, 43, 49, 55.
27. 53 and 54. Top sequence: add 9, 7, etc. Bottom sequence: add 7, 9, etc.
28. 29 and 27. Top sequence: subtract 4, 5, etc. Bottom sequence: subtract 5, 6, etc.
29. 127 and 122. Top sequence: × 3 − 1 at each stage. Bottom sequence: × 2 + 1 at each stage.
30. 11 and 13. In each sequence add the previous two numbers to obtain the next number.

## Assessment

Score 1 point for each correct answer.

| | |
|---|---|
| 12–17 | Average |
| 18–23 | Good |
| 24–27 | Very good |
| 28–30 | Exceptional |

Transfer your score to the tests of numerical aptitude overall assessment chart on page 102.

## Answers to Test two

1. 45 2. 24 3. 56 4. 98 5. 84 6. 77 7. 165 8. 27 9. 171 10. 81 11. 9 12. 114 13. 72 14. 56 15. 108 16. 160 17. 733 18. 923 19. 1,080 20. 205 21. 20.54 22. 1,170 23. 12.5 24. 0.1875 25. 1,251 26. 1,014 27. 423 28. 148.5 29. 54 30. 51,279

## Assessment

Score 1 point for each correct answer.

| | |
|---|---|
| 12–17 | Average |
| 18–23 | Good |
| 24–27 | Very good |
| 28–30 | Exceptional |

Transfer your score to the tests of numerical aptitude overall assessment chart on page 102.

## Answers to Test three

1. 8  2. 1  3. 8  4. 0  5. 7  6. b  7. e  8. d  9. a  10. e  11. d  12. e  13. c  14. b  15. d

## Assessment

Score 1 point for each correct answer.

| | |
|---|---|
| 6–7 | Average |
| 8–10 | Good |
| 11–12 | Very good |
| 13–15 | Exceptional |

Transfer your score to the tests of numerical aptitude overall assessment chart on page 102.

## Answers to Test four

1. 7
2. 

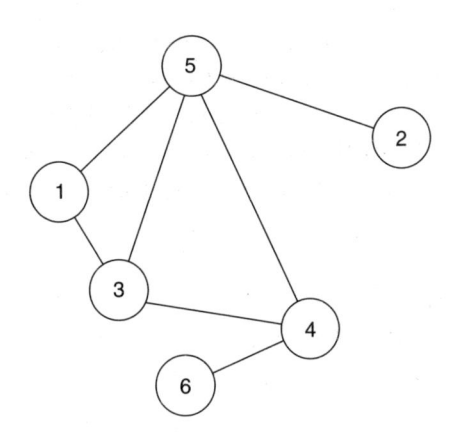

[Diagram showing circles numbered 1-6 connected: 5 connects to 1, 3, 4, 2; 1 connects to 3; 3 connects to 4; 4 connects to 6]

3. 113
    86 + 27 = 113
4. Harry is 32, Carrie is 40 and Barry is 50.
5. 31

    $$\frac{(3 \times 7) + (9 \times 8)}{\sqrt[3]{(3 \times 9)}}$$

6. 56 minutes
7. 

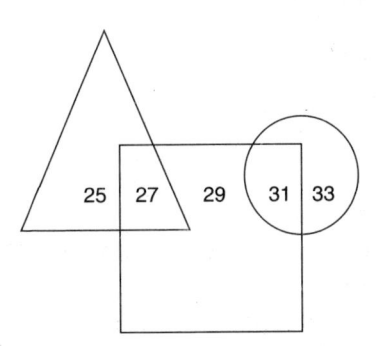

[Diagram showing a triangle, square, and circle overlapping with numbers 25, 27, 29, 31, 33 arranged horizontally; 25 inside triangle only; 27 inside triangle and square; 29 inside square only; 31 inside square and circle; 33 inside circle only]

8. 60. 11 am to 12 noon = 99 e-mails, which is 65% more than 60.
9. £65.79
    86 − 10% = 77.40
    77.40 − 15% = 65.79

10. 1 hour 55 minutes
    49 + 49 + 17
11. 72 (9 × 8)
12. 1. In each line across and down, the total of the first two numbers equals the total of the second two numbers.
13. £112.91. Train = £89.65, taxi = £21.38 and bus = £1.88.
14. 24. Take the difference between the number formed by the first two digits and the number formed by the second two digits.
15. 55
    (6 + 3 + 2) × 5
16. c. 4853 : 3215 : 65
    4 × 8 = 32 and 5 × 3 = 15
    3 × 2 = 6 and 1 × 5 = 5
17. 0.40

    $\frac{3}{9} \times \frac{6}{5}$

18. 30 cm
    By Pythagoras:

    6,084 − 5,184 = 900

    78 × 78 = 6,084

    less: 72 × 72 = $\frac{5,184}{900}$

    √900 = 30
19. 65. Add 10, 11, 12, 13, 14.
20. 9. Looking down each column: 287 + 594 = 881; therefore 329 + 597 = 926.
21. −13. The rule is to replace − − with +
    −45 + 32 = −13
22. 50 minutes
    8 × 75 = 600
    8 + 4 = 12
    600 ÷ 12 = 50 minutes

23. 4,186
    7,774 ÷ 13 = 598
    598 × 7 = 4,186
24. −21
    The rule is to replace + − with −
    −16 − 5 = −21
25. 2,260
    (339 ÷ 15) × 100

## Assessment

Score 1 point for each correct answer.

|  |  |
|---|---|
| 10–13 | Average |
| 14–17 | Good |
| 18–22 | Very good |
| 23–25 | Exceptional |

Transfer your score to the tests of numerical aptitude overall assessment chart on page 102.

## Tests of numerical aptitude: overall assessment

| Test | Description | Score |
|---|---|---|
| One | Sequences | |
| Two | Mental arithmetic test | |
| Three | Complete the equation test | |
| Four | General numerical test | |
| Total score | | |

A total of 100 points is available in this chapter.

| | |
|---|---|
| 32–48 | Average |
| 49–78 | Good |
| 79–88 | Very good |
| 89–100 | Exceptional |

Divide your score by 2, round up to the nearest whole number and transfer the result to the overall brain quotient (BQ) rating chart on page 227.

# Tests of spatial aptitude

The definition of *spatial* is 'pertaining to space', and spatial abilities mean the perceptual and cognitive abilities that enable a person to deal with spatial relations.

This type of abstract reasoning does not involve problems that are verbal or numerical in nature. The questions within such tests typically take the form of a series of shapes or diagrams from which you have to pick the odd one out, or you have to identify which should come next in a sequence from a set of alternatives, or choose from a set of alternatives which diagram will complete an analogy. The ability being investigated in this type of test is how well a person is able to identify patterns and meaning from what might appear at first glance random or very complex information.

Such tests are referred to as culture-free or culture-fair tests, and are designed to be free of any cultural bias, so that no advantage is derived by individuals of one culture relative to those of another. In other words, they eliminate language factors or other skills that might be closely tied to one particular culture.

## Test one: box clever test

You have 40 minutes in which to complete this test.

1.

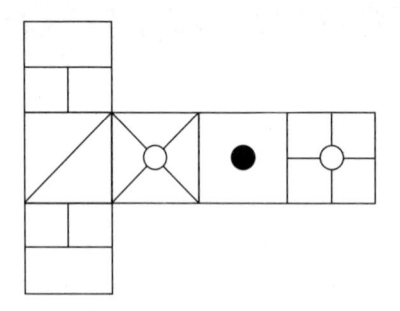

When the above is folded to form a cube, just one of the following can be produced. Which one?

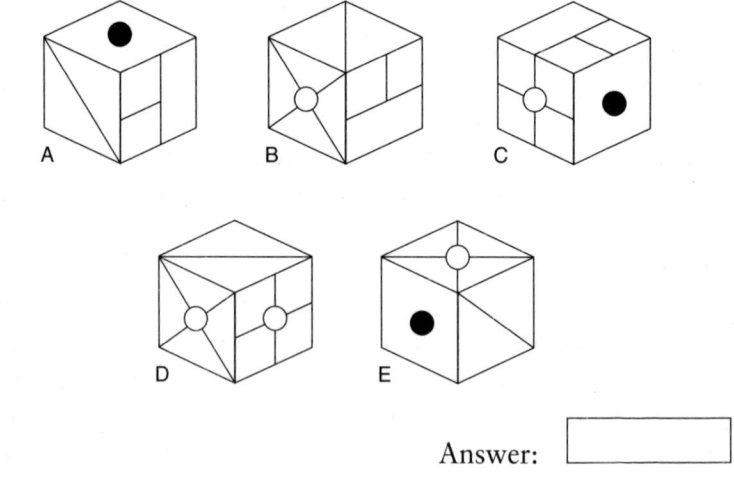

Answer:

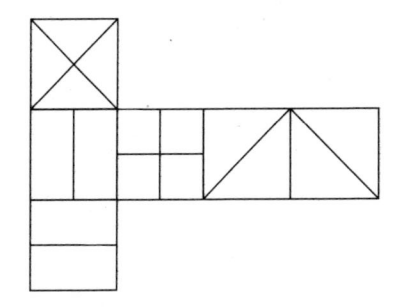

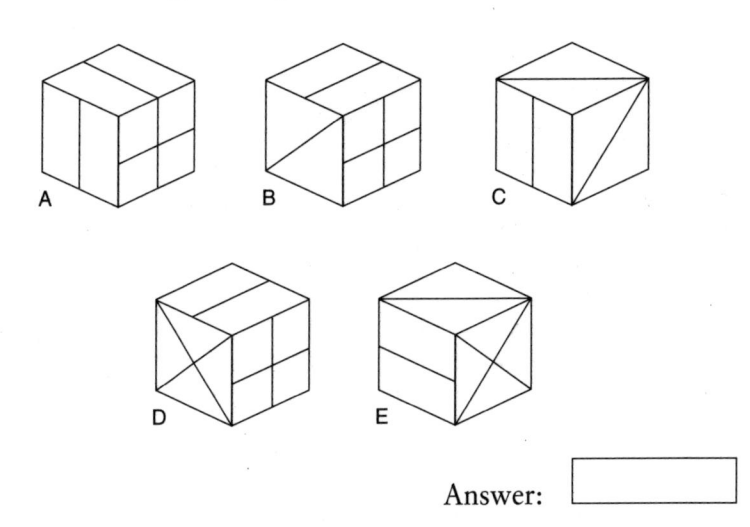

2.

When the above is folded to form a cube, just one of the following can be produced. Which one?

A  B  C

D  E

Answer:

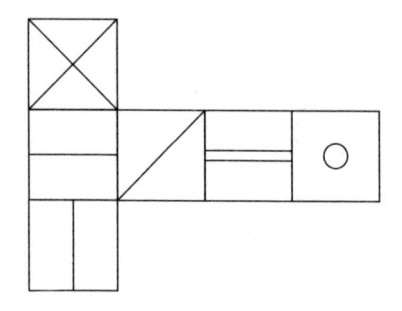

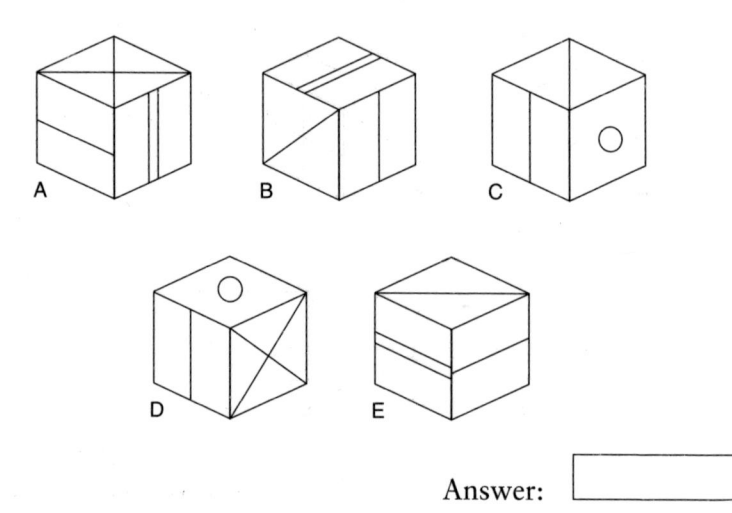

3.

When the above is folded to form a cube, just one of the following can be produced. Which one?

Answer:

4.

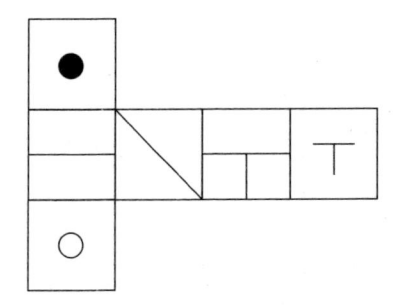

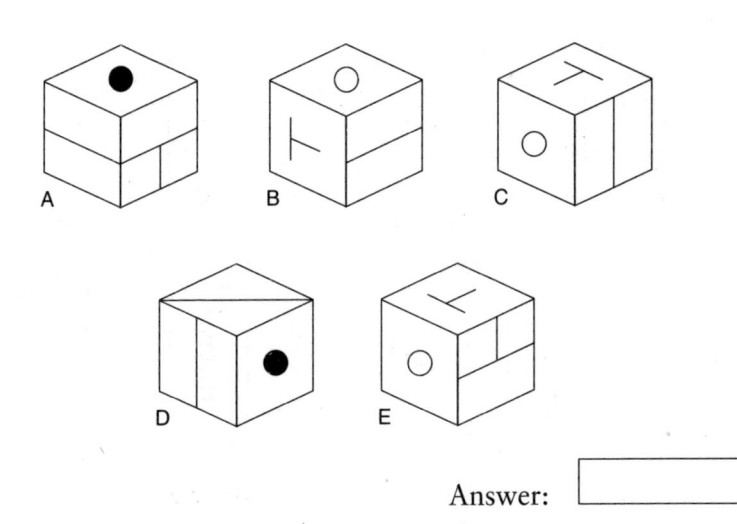

When the above is folded to form a cube, just one of the following can be produced. Which one?

Answer:

5.

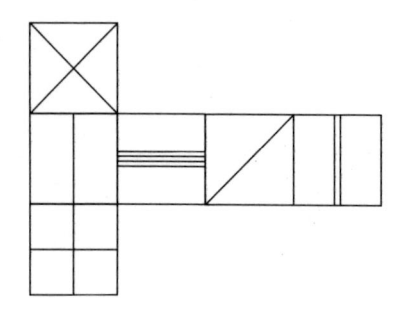

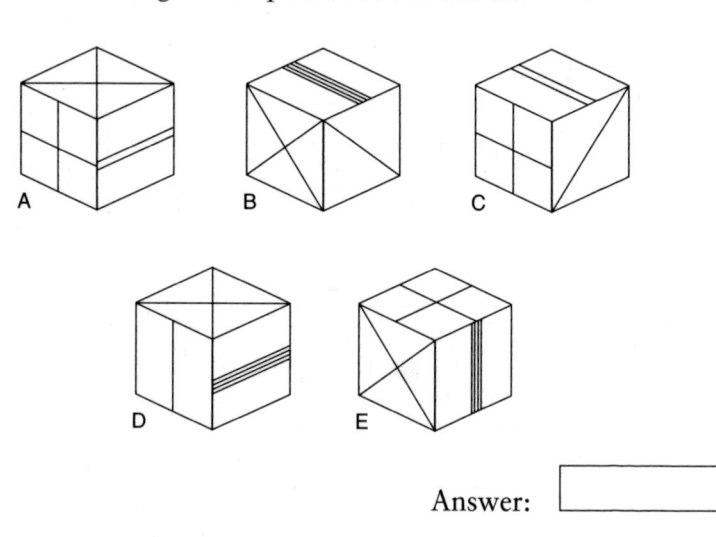

When the above is folded to form a cube, just one of the following can be produced. Which one?

Answer:

6.

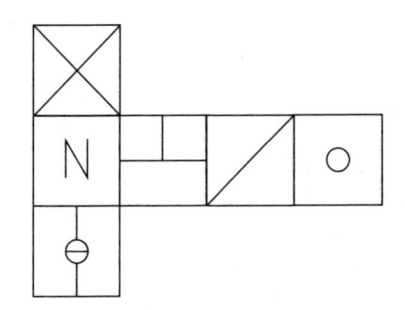

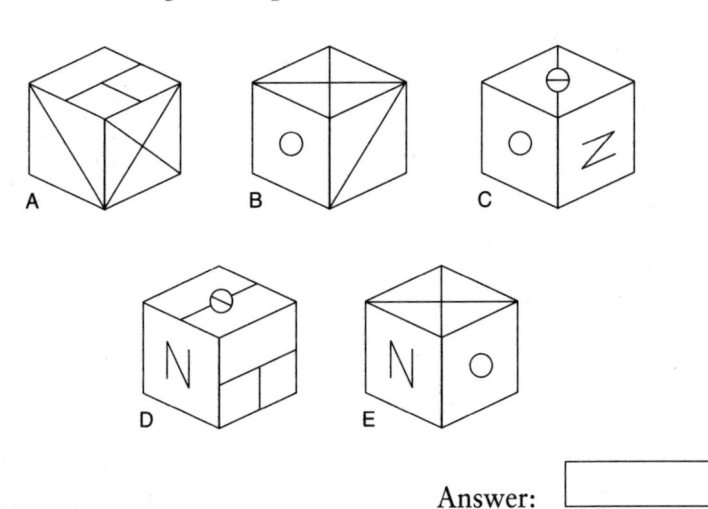

When the above is folded to form a cube, just one of the following can be produced. Which one?

Answer:

7.

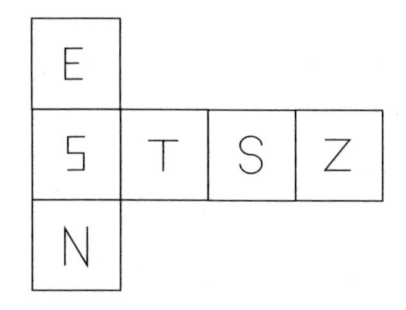

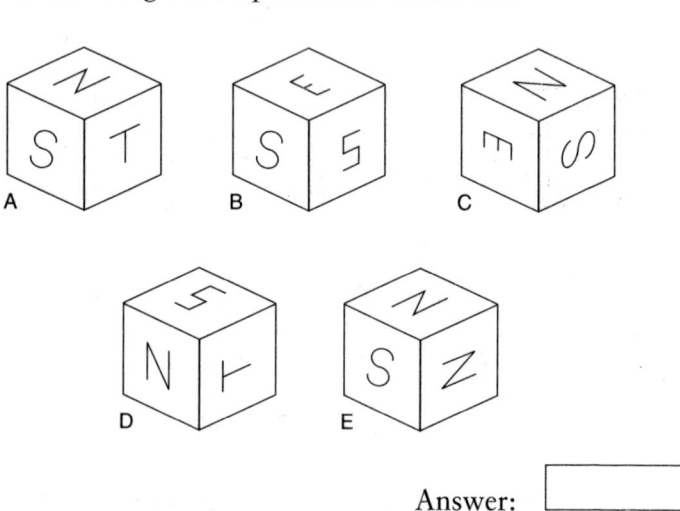

|   | E |   |   |
|---|---|---|---|
| 5 | T | S | Z |
|   | N |   |   |

When the above is folded to form a cube, just one of the following can be produced. Which one?

A  B  C

D  E

Answer:

8.

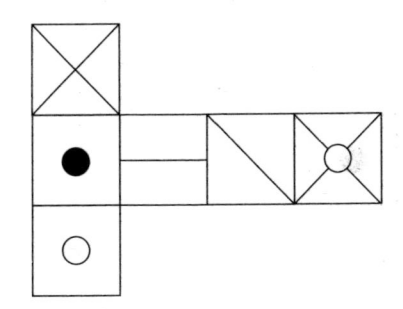

When the above is folded to form a cube, which is the only one of the following that cannot be produced?

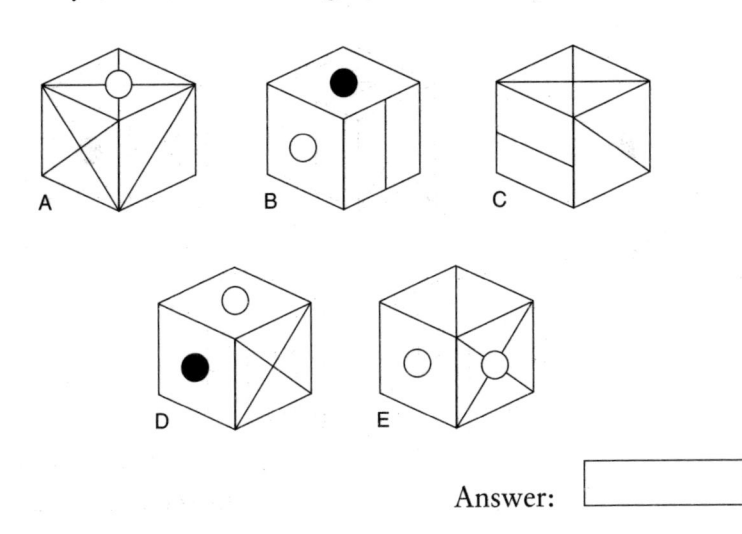

Answer: [          ]

112  Test and assess your brain quotient

9.

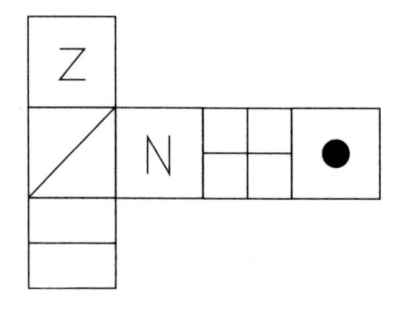

When the above is folded to form a cube, which is the only one of the following that cannot be produced?

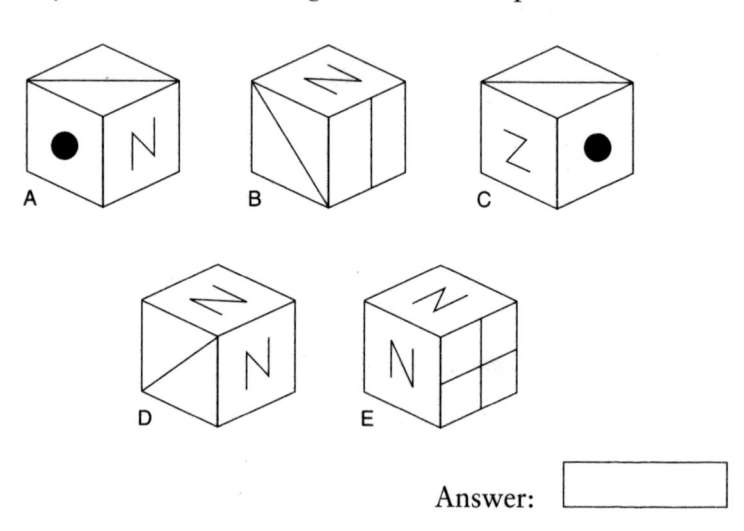

Answer: ☐

10.

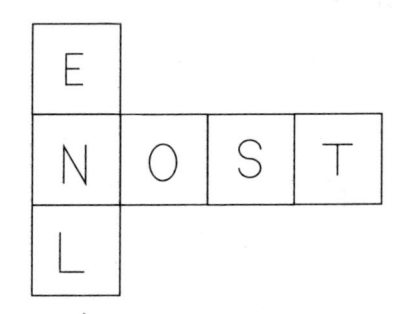

| | E | | | |
|---|---|---|---|---|
| N | O | S | T | |
| | L | | | |

When the above is folded to form a cube, which is the only one of the following that cannot be produced?

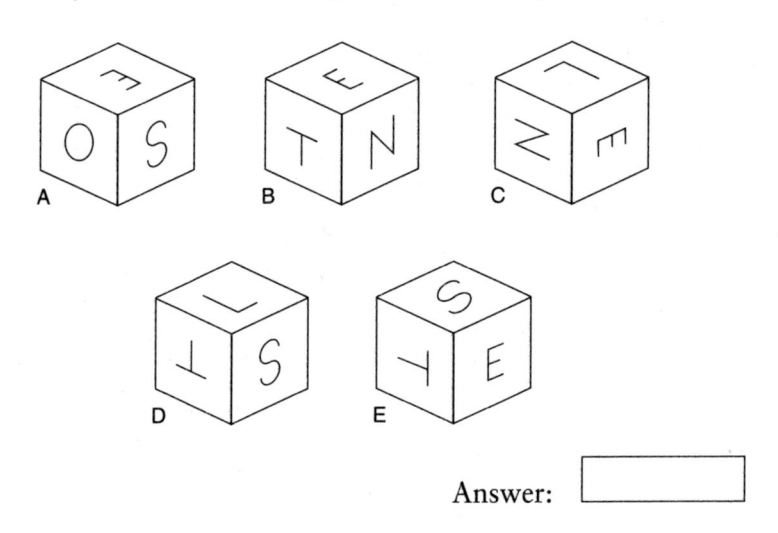

A  B  C

D  E

Answer:

114  Test and assess your brain quotient

# Test two: general test

You have 60 minutes in which to solve the 15 questions.

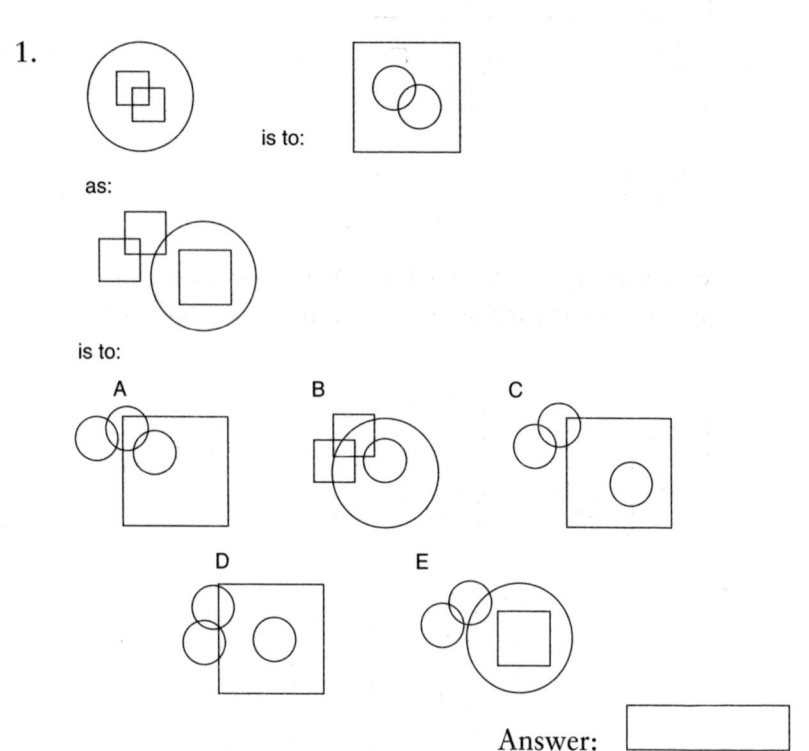

1. ⊙ is to: ▭

as:

▭⊙ is to:

A  B  C
D  E

Answer: ☐

Tests of spatial aptitude 115

2.

What comes next?

A  B  C

D  E

Answer:

3.

is to:

as:

is to:

A  B  C

D  E

Answer:

4.

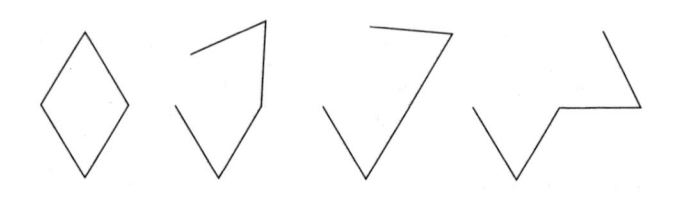

What comes next?

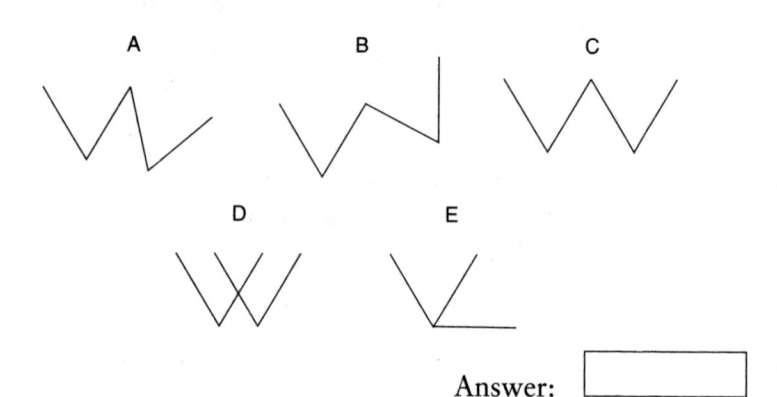

A   B   C

D   E

Answer: ☐

5.

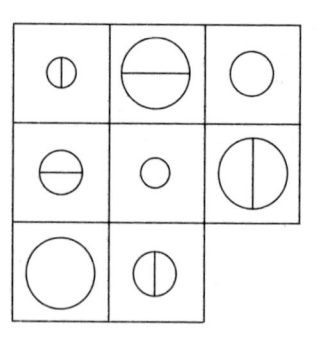

Which tile should complete the matrix?

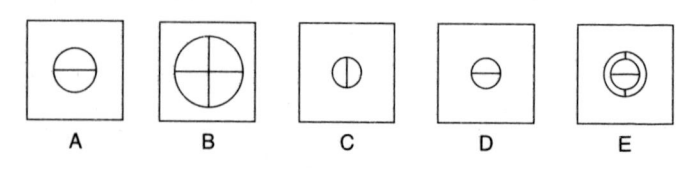

A   B   C   D   E

Answer: ☐

# Tests of spatial aptitude 117

6.

What comes next?

Answer:

7.

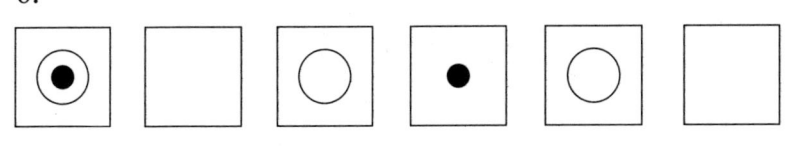

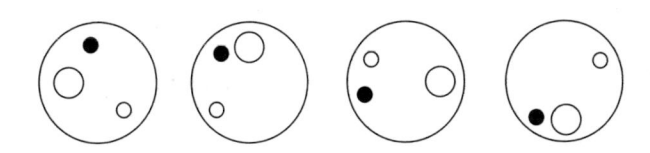

What comes next?

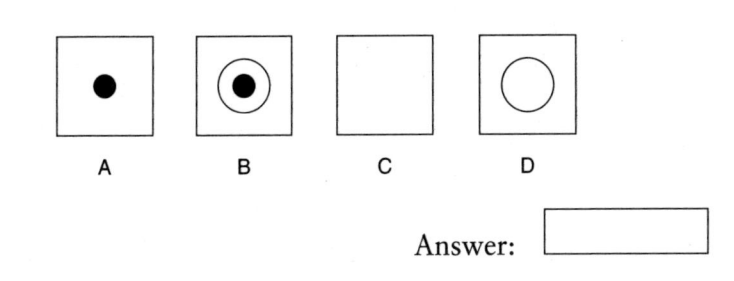

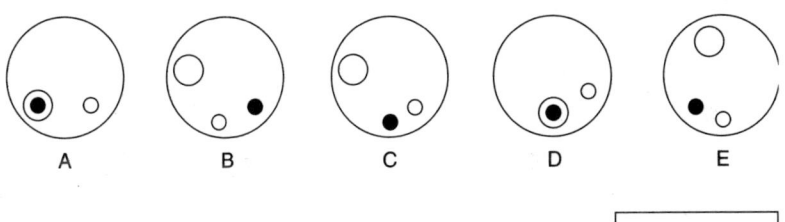

Answer:

118 Test and assess your brain quotient

8.

is to:

as:

is to:

A     B     C

D     E

Answer: ☐

9.

What comes next?

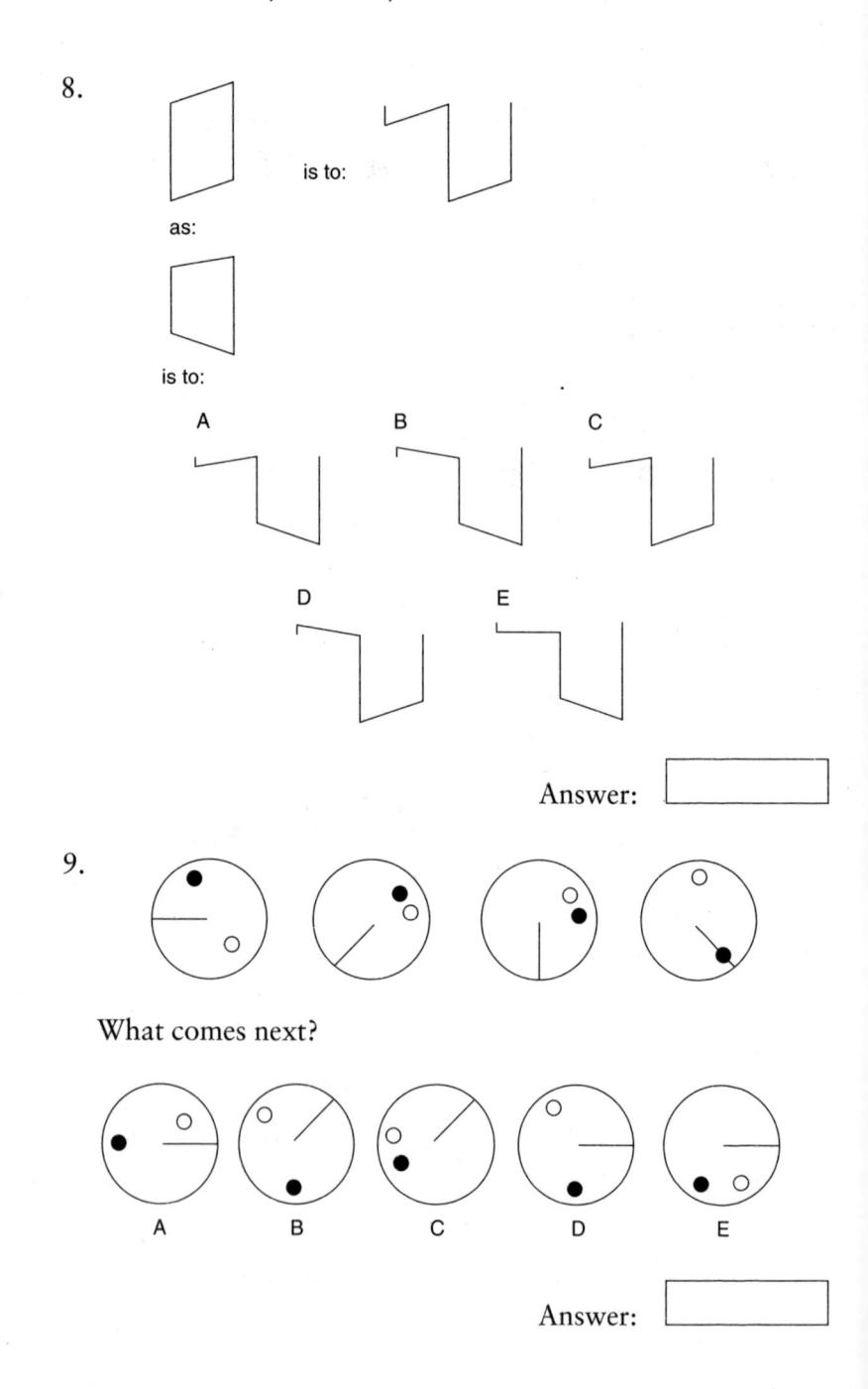

A   B   C   D   E

Answer: ☐

Tests of spatial aptitude 119

10.

is to:

as:

is to:

A    B    C

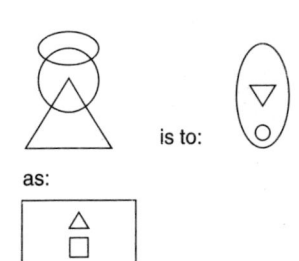

D    E

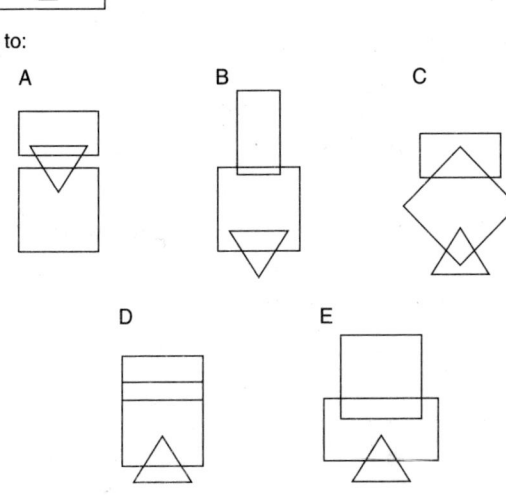

Answer:

11. Which is the odd one out?

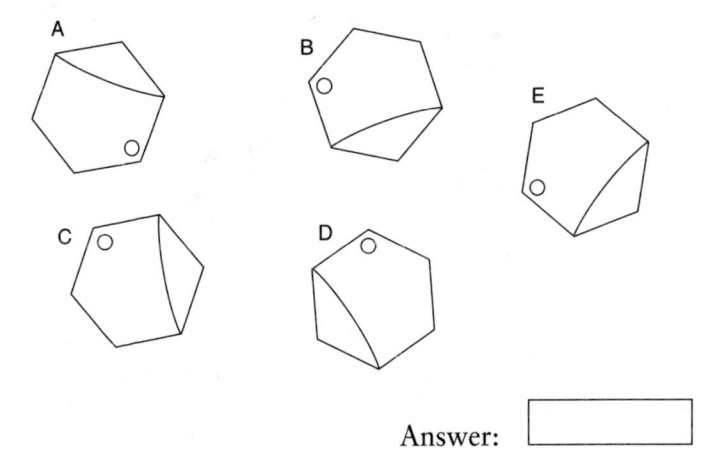

A   B   E   C   D

Answer:

120  Test and assess your brain quotient

12.

What comes next?

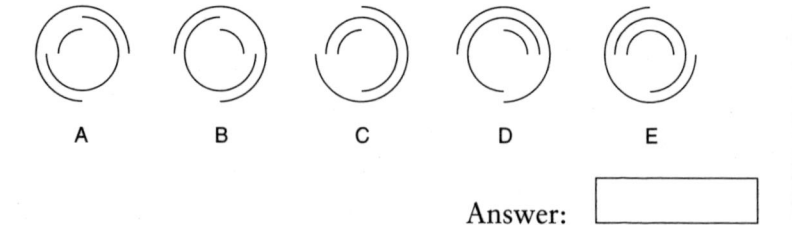

A   B   C   D   E

Answer: 

13. Which is the odd one out?

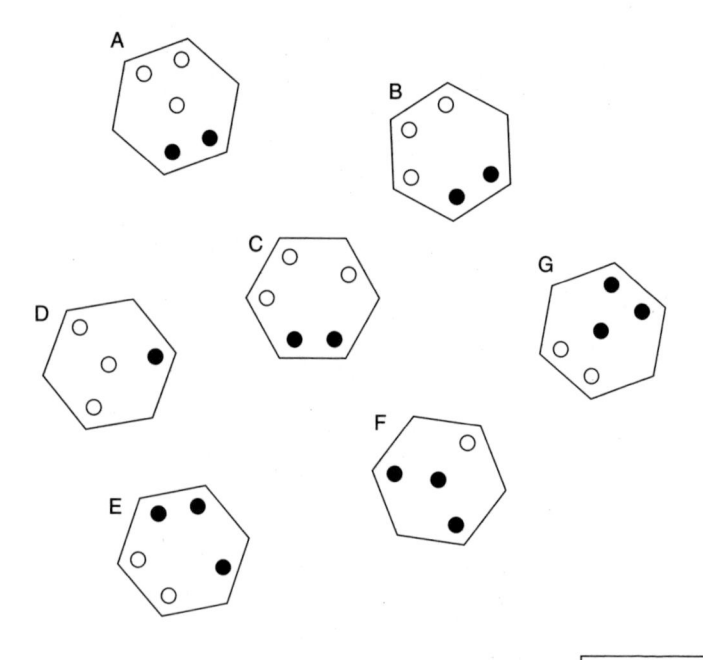

Answer:

14.

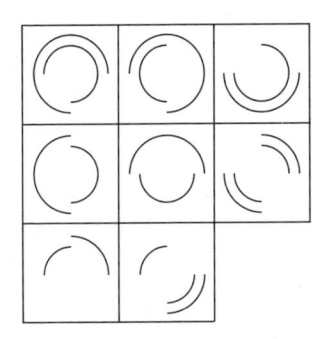

Which tile should complete the matrix?

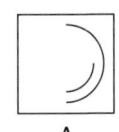

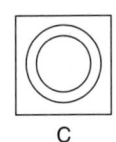

A  B  C  D  E

Answer:

122　Test and assess your brain quotient

15.

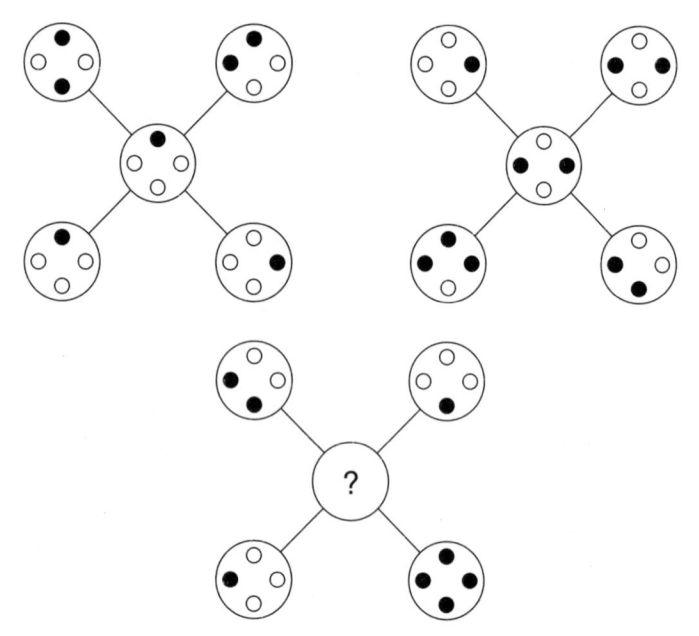

Which option below should replace the question mark?

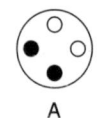

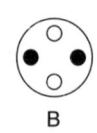

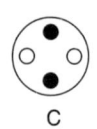

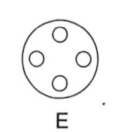

A　B　C　D　E

Answer: ☐

## Answers to Test one

1. B 2. E 3. D 4. C 5. D 6. A 7. C 8. D 9. A 10. C

## Assessment

Score 1 point for each correct answer.

| | |
|---|---|
| 4–5 | Average |
| 6–7 | Good |
| 8 | Very good |
| 9–10 | Exceptional |

Transfer your score to the tests of spatial aptitude overall assessment chart on page 125.

## Answers to Test two

1. C. Circles change to squares and vice versa.
2. E. At each stage the number of black dots increases by one and the number of white dots decreases by one.
3. E. The figure rotates 90° clockwise.
4. B. The two lines at the top are moving 45° clockwise at each stage.
5. D. Looking across and down, each line contains one of each size circle and a vertical and horizontal line.
6. B. Every alternate box contains a circle and every third box contains a dot.
7. C. The black dot is moving 45° anticlockwise at each stage, the circle is moving 90° clockwise at each stage and the white dot is moving 90° clockwise at each stage.
8. A. The top bit flips over to the left
9. D. The black dot moves 45° clockwise at each stage, the line moves 45° anticlockwise at each stage and the white dot moves 45° anticlockwise at each stage.

10. B. Reversing the movement of the example, the rectangle rotates 90° and goes to the top, the square increases in size and goes in the middle and the triangle increases in size, rotates 180° and goes to the bottom.
11. C. The rest are the same figure rotated.
12. D. The outer arc rotates 90° clockwise, the middle arc rotates 90° clockwise and the inner arc rotates 90° anticlockwise.
13. B. A is the same as G with black/white reversal, as are C and E, and D and F.
14. D. In each row and column combine the first and second tiles to produce the contents of the third tile, but cancel out common lines.
15. A. Only when a dot appears in the same position three times in the four surrounding circles is it transferred to the middle circle.

## Assessment

Score 1 point for each correct answer.

| | |
|---|---|
| 6–7 | Average |
| 8–10 | Good |
| 11–12 | Very good |
| 13–15 | Exceptional |

Transfer your score to the tests of spatial aptitude overall assessment chart on page 125.

## Tests of spatial aptitude: overall assessment

| Test | Description | Score |
|------|-------------|-------|
| One | Box clever test | |
| Two | General test | |
| Total score | | |

A total of 25 points is available in this chapter.

| | |
|---|---|
| 10–13 | Average |
| 14–17 | Good |
| 18–22 | Very good |
| 23–25 | Exceptional |

Multiply your score by 2 and transfer the result to the overall brain quotient (BQ) rating chart on page 227.

# 6
# *Personality questionnaires*

Emotional intelligence, more commonly referred to as EQ (emotional quotient), is the ability to be aware of one's own emotions and those of other people. The two main aspects of EQ are: understanding yourself and your goals, aspirations, responses and behaviour; and understanding others and their feelings.

The concept of emotional intelligence was developed in the mid-1990s by Daniel Goleman, coming to prominence with his 1995 book *Emotional Intelligence*. The early emotional intelligence theory was developed in the United States during the 1970s and 1980s by the work and writings of Howard Gardner of Harvard University, Peter Salovey (Yale) and John Mayer (New Hampshire).

In general, the term *personality* refers to the patterns of thought, feeling and behaviour that are unique in every one of us, and these are the characteristics that distinguish us from other people. Our personality thus implies the predictability of how we are likely to act or react under different circumstances.

It is now widely recognized that if someone is deemed intellectually intelligent it does not necessarily follow that he or she is also emotionally intelligent. Being intellectually brilliant does not mean that a person is able to relate to other people socially, nor does it mean that a person is capable of managing his or her own emotions or able to motivate him- or herself.

The following questionnaires are designed to test different aspects of your personality. The procedure for completing each of these is to answer the questions as truthfully and as realistically as possible; in other words, be true to yourself at all times in order to obtain the most accurate assessment.

There is no need to read through these tests first before attempting them: just answer intuitively and without too much consideration. There are no right or wrong answers, and although you should work as quickly as possible there is no set time limit.

## Test one: attitude

Answer each question or statement by choosing which one of the three responses given is most applicable to you.

1. It is fair to describe the vast majority of people as basically decent.

    a. I would say the majority, but not the vast majority
    b. Not particularly in my experience
    c. Yes

    Answer:

2. Do you always try to see the other person's point of view?

    a. Not always, but sometimes it is the best way to resolve a problem
    b. It is a waste of time if the person holding a diametrically opposing viewpoint to mine is obviously wrong
    c. In almost all instances it is desirable to do so

    Answer:

3. How important is it for you to keep a tidy house and garden?

   a. More desirable than important
   b. It is not one of my great priorities in life, as a house should look lived in
   c. Very important

   Answer: [ ]

4. How proud are you of your nationality?

   a. More pleased than proud
   b. Not very proud at all
   c. Very proud

   Answer: [ ]

5. I feel good when I know that other people like and respect me?

   a. Agree
   b. It doesn't really concern me, as I am my own person
   c. Agree strongly

   Answer: [ ]

6. Do you believe that revenge is sweet?

   a. It can be
   b. Yes
   c. No; if someone does you a bad turn just move on from it

   Answer: [ ]

7. How easy is it for you to forgive and forget?

    a. It depends on what I am forgiving
    b. I find it difficult to forgive and forget
    c. Quite easy

    Answer:

8. Would you say that communication is one of your strong points?

    a. I would like to think so
    b. Not sure
    c. Most certainly

    Answer:

9. You are out walking the dog on the moors and a stranger is approaching, also walking a dog. What is likely to be your reaction?

    a. I may pass the time of day with the person
    b. Probably speak if I am spoken to
    c. I would almost always pass the time of day

    Answer:

10. Do you think it is important to make a good impression when meeting other people?

    a. Sometimes
    b. Not really; people will have to take me as they find me
    c. I would try to be polite and courteous with them, which I hope will make a good impression

    Answer:

11. Do you tend to react differently to people depending on their status or authority?

    a. Sometimes, if it is to my advantage to do so
    b. Yes
    c. No

    Answer:

12. How eager are you to please others?

    a. I don't go out of my way to please others
    b. Not particularly eager
    c. My main priority is to please myself, and by doing so it may well please others

    Answer:

13. How keen are you to keep yourself fit and active?

    a. Fairly keen
    b. It is not something I give a great deal of thought to
    c. It is something I attach a lot of importance to

    Answer:

14. Do you believe that the more we put into society the more we get out of it?

    a. Perhaps
    b. Not necessarily – sometimes we don't get enough reward for the good things we do in life
    c. Yes

    Answer:

15. How important do you feel it is to judge people on first appearances?

    a. In many cases first appearances tell you a great deal about a person you are meeting for the first time
    b. Very important
    c. It is a mistake to try to judge people on first appearances

    Answer: [ ]

16. Do you consider yourself a lucky person?

    a. Luck evens itself out – probably I'm no luckier or unluckier than the next person
    b. No
    c. Yes

    Answer: [ ]

17. Is it important to meet agreed deadlines?

    a. Not terribly important – the most important thing is to do a good job of work in your own time
    b. The only thing I like about deadlines is the whooshing sound they make as they rush by
    c. Very important

    Answer: [ ]

18. You are running for a bus that you need to catch to meet an urgent appointment when someone passing you, going the other way, trips and crashes full length on to the pavement. What would you do?

    a. That is one of those circumstances where I couldn't really be sure what I would do until the situation actually arose
    b. As there would be plenty of other people around who would render assistance I would, under the circumstances, carry on and catch the bus
    c. Stop and render assistance even if this meant missing the bus and my appointment

    Answer: [ ]

19. How worried are you about the level of crime in our society?

    a. It does concern me to a certain extent
    b. It doesn't concern me
    c. I am worried and concerned

    Answer: [ ]

20. Do you continually look forward to, and plan for, the future?

    a. I do try to plan for the future in certain respects
    b. Not particularly
    c. Yes

    Answer: [ ]

21. You are fitting a new external door for someone, but it is taking longer than expected and your partner is cooking you a meal for 5 pm. It is now 4.30 pm and the job will take another two hours to complete. What would you do?

    a. Ask if the person would mind if I called it a day and returned tomorrow; however, if the person expressed disappointment I would finish the job
    b. Explain that I have to leave the job unfinished as my partner has prepared a meal, but promise that I will return tomorrow
    c. Phone my partner to explain I will be late and finish the job

    Answer:

22. How often have you carried out voluntary work?

    a. Occasionally
    b. Rarely or never
    c. Often

    Answer:

23. What are your views on global warming?

    a. It exists but there isn't much that can be done about it
    b. It is an exaggerated problem
    c. It is a serious problem for future generations

    Answer:

24. Do you tend to complain a lot?

    a.  I certainly complain when I feel it is necessary to do so
    b.  If by that you mean do I complain when there is something to complain about – then the answer is probably yes
    c.  Not really

    Answer: [ ]

25. It is the responsibility of parents to teach their children the difference between right and wrong from a very early age

    a.  Most parents do their best and it is often all too easy to blame the parents for their children's behaviour
    b.  Often things are not that simple – it isn't always possible for parents to teach their children right or wrong, for a variety of reasons
    c.  Agree emphatically

    Answer: [ ]

## Test two: success factor

Answer each question or statement by choosing which one of the three responses given is most applicable to you.

1.  How happy are you in the job you are doing?

    a.  Not very happy
    b.  Very happy
    c.  I can put up with it – it's a living

    Answer: [ ]

2. Are you able to express your thoughts and feelings to others?

   a. It is something that I often find difficult to do
   b. Yes
   c. Most of the time, but not always

   Answer:

3. To what extent do you consider it is worth taking risks to fulfil your ambitions?

   a. I think it is unwise to take risks with something as important as your career
   b. You have certainly got to take risks at times if you wish to fulfil your ambitions
   c. I don't mind taking the occasional calculated risk

   Answer:

4. Would you describe yourself as a doer or a thinker?

   a. A thinker
   b. Both a doer and a thinker
   c. A doer

   Answer:

5. It is important to finish what you start.

   a. Not necessarily – sometimes it is prudent to abandon even the best of intentions
   b. I agree
   c. You should always try to finish what you start if possible

   Answer:

6. To what extent do you think it is possible to achieve a high level of success without the involvement of others?

   a. It is quite possible – there are many self-made people
   b. I believe it is highly unlikely that anyone is able to achieve a high level of success without the involvement of others
   c. It is possible, but usually you do need some degree of involvement from other people

   Answer:

7. Do you consider yourself ruthless?

   a. No
   b. Yes, I can be ruthless when it comes to getting what I want
   c. I would hope that people do not perceive me as being a ruthless person

   Answer:

8. In life you make most of your own luck – be it good or bad.

   a. I disagree – if fate wants to deal you a bad or a good hand it will do so
   b. I agree
   c. You make some of your own luck, but fate also has a big part to play

   Answer:

9. People who are continually boasting about their achievements do so in order to disguise their own feelings of insecurity.

   a. Disagree
   b. Agree
   c. Not sure

   Answer: [ ]

10. How ambitious do you consider yourself to be?

    a. Not very ambitious
    b. Very ambitious
    c. I have hopes and aspirations rather than ambitions

    Answer: [ ]

11. Are you afraid of failure?

    a. Yes
    b. No
    c. It is something I have never really thought about

    Answer: [ ]

12. Do you know where you want to be in five years' time?

    a. No, I prefer to live for the present
    b. Yes
    c. Yes, I want to be alive and kicking

    Answer: [ ]

13. Have you ever suffered from some degree of inferiority complex?

    a. I think so
    b. No
    c. Not that I am aware of

    Answer: [ ]

14. You have to make things happen.

    a. Disagree – let fate take a hand
    b. Agree
    c. Sometimes

    Answer: [ ]

15. What motivates you the greatest?

    a. My desire for a stable and content lifestyle
    b. My own personal desires and ambitions
    c. The desire to make money

    Answer: [ ]

16. In your working life, do you usually expect to be considered for a promotion when the opportunity arises?

    a. No, as this means that you are not disappointed when it doesn't happen
    b. Yes
    c. Sometimes, but not always, as I like to keep my aspirations within attainable limits

    Answer: [ ]

17. With which of the following statements do you agree the most?

    a. A team is at its strongest when it is working well within itself
    b. A team can only be at its strongest when its purpose is in line with all its members' wants and needs
    c. A team is at its strongest when clear objectives are set

    Answer:

18. You are in a safe and secure job with a decent salary when you are suddenly headhunted by another organization offering you a higher salary and more responsibility. What decision would you most likely reach about your future?

    a. I would not risk leaving a safe job in such circumstances
    b. I would take the new job
    c. Not sure; it is something I would have to think long and hard about

    Answer:

19. Do you feel that you are stuck in a rut?

    a. Yes
    b. No
    c. Sometimes

    Answer:

20. Hard work brings its rewards.

    a. Disagree
    b. Agree
    c. Hard work usually means success for others and not the person who does all the hard work

    Answer:

21. Do you think that a high level of intelligence leads to success?

    a. A high level of intelligence is a crucial factor on the road to success
    b. It might help but it is only a small part of what is necessary to make someone successful
    c. A high degree of intelligence can sometimes be a hindrance to success

    Answer:

22. How easy is it for you to channel all your energies into just one task?

    a. Quite difficult, as I like to diversify my interests
    b. I have no difficulties in this respect
    c. Not all that easy, but with a certain amount of effort and concentration it is possible

    Answer:

23. Have you ever had a hobby that has interfered with your day job?

    a. Yes
    b. No
    c. Perhaps to a small degree

    Answer:

24. Would you describe yourself as a try, try and try again person?

    a. Life's too short to pursue lost causes
    b. Yes, I don't give up a cause easily
    c. Sometimes it is worth the effort to keep persevering

    Answer:

25. Would you be prepared to give up a hobby you love dearly if it meant achieving success in your chosen career?

    a. No, I value my leisure too highly to give something up that I love doing dearly
    b. Certainly
    c. Not sure about giving it up completely but I might be prepared to scale down the hobby, as I believe there is room for both

    Answer: ☐

## Test three: how imaginative are you?

Answer each question or statement by choosing which one of the three responses given is most applicable to you.

1. Which of the following most closely represents your attitude to change?

    a. It is inevitable and is sometimes an exciting new challenge
    b. Change is more often for the worse and not for the better
    c. It is something we all have to try to accept and move along with

    Answer: ☐

2. Which of the following is your favourite type of book?

    a. Murder, mystery and suspense
    b. An autobiography
    c. An encyclopedia

    Answer: ☐

3. Which of the following best represents your views on the old adage 'There is a time and place for everything'?

    a. It's all too regimented for me
    b. Generally agree
    c. Maybe it is relevant in certain situations

    Answer: [    ]

4. How strongly do you rely on your intuition?

    a. Quite a lot
    b. I prefer to make decisions based on logic rather than intuition
    c. Occasionally

    Answer: [    ]

5. Given the choice of holiday, which of these would you prefer?

    a. An adventure holiday in the Swiss Alps
    b. Sun and sangria on the Costa del Sol
    c. A trip to Las Vegas

    Answer: [    ]

6. Which of the following is your favourite type of garden?

    a. Wild woodland
    b. Formal flower beds around a well-manicured lawn
    c. Large lawn surrounded by a herbaceous border

    Answer: [    ]

7. Have you ever had an idea for something that you believe would make a great invention?

   a. Yes, on several occasions
   b. Nothing springs to mind
   c. I did have a couple of ideas at one time but wasn't sure how to go about developing them

   Answer:

8. Do you enjoy tinkering about with things and repairing them?

   a. Yes, very much so
   b. Oh no, I'm hopeless at anything like that
   c. I wouldn't say I enjoy it, but I can turn my hand to one or two things if necessary

   Answer:

9. What is your opinion of modern art?

   a. It interests me
   b. Most of it is totally absurd
   c. Not for me, but it wouldn't do for everyone to have the same taste in art

   Answer:

10. Do you ever feel frustrated that you could be doing something much more interesting and challenging with your life?

    a. Yes, frequently
    b. No, I'm generally content with things as they are
    c. Only very occasionally

    Answer:

11. Out of the following, which would you like to cultivate as a new pursuit or hobby?

    a. Painting
    b. Golf
    c. Collecting antiques

    Answer: [ ]

12. Do you like exploring the world of computers?

    a. Yes
    b. I cannot say I have much interest in computers
    c. I do what I need to do on computers and that's it

    Answer: [ ]

13. Are computers an exciting new challenge or a necessary evil?

    a. An exciting new challenge
    b. Are they even necessary?
    c. A necessary evil

    Answer: [ ]

14. Do you believe in the paranormal?

    a. Yes
    b. No
    c. I have an open mind on the subject

    Answer: [ ]

15. Which of the following most takes your breath away?

    a. A golden eagle in free flight
    b. A great operatic voice
    c. A natural wonder such as the Grand Canyon

    Answer: [ ]

16. Do you like to doodle?

    a. Yes, I often find myself doodling
    b. No, I rarely or never find myself doodling
    c. Sometimes

    Answer:

17. How often do you fantasize?

    a. Frequently
    b. Rarely or never
    c. Occasionally

    Answer:

18. Which of the following is most likely to be the reason why you could not get to sleep at night?

    a. An overactive mind
    b. Not being tired
    c. Worry

    Answer:

19. What is your opinion of graffiti?

    a. Although it is not really desirable, some of it is quite artistic
    b. It is something that should be prosecuted more often and stiffer penalties imposed for the perpetrators
    c. It's a pity people cannot channel their creativity into something more worthwhile

    Answer:

20. Do you believe it is necessary to conform in order to be accepted?

    a. Most definitely not, and why should it be?
    b. Yes, to a great extent it is necessary
    c. It shouldn't be necessary, but in many circumstances it is

    Answer:

21. Which of the following would you choose on a day out?

    a. Struggling to find my way round Hampton Court Maze
    b. A day out at my favourite seaside resort
    c. A long walk in the country

    Answer:

22. If you won £1 million on the lottery, which of the following statements would most sum up your feelings?

    a. Now I can do all the things I always wanted to do
    b. Now I can retire and live a life of luxurious leisure
    c. I can invest in a new business venture

    Answer:

23. Are you a dedicated follower of fashion?

    a. No, I prefer to do my own thing within reason
    b. Yes, I like to keep abreast of, and follow, the latest fashions
    c. I like to dress in clothes that I consider smart, comfortable and not too outdated

    Answer:

24. Which of the following words appeals to you the most?

   a. free
   b. formidable
   c. flexible

   Answer:

25. You are out with friends for a celebratory meal. Which of the following would you be most likely to choose?

   a. Something new, but highly recommended, for the main course
   b. Something you know you like to eat
   c. Something new for the dessert course only

   Answer:

## Assessment for Test one

Award yourself 2 points for every 'c' answer, 1 point for every 'a', and 0 points for every 'b'.

## Analysis

Attitudes are not something with which we are born. They can be formed and developed in many different ways, for example by the influences in our lives, such as parents, with whom many people hold the same beliefs.

The attitudes of individuals can change throughout their lifetime. These changes may be as a result of prevailing circumstances or life's experiences: hence the phrase *developing an attitude*. These changes may be positive, in which case the individual can develop a better attitude, or negative, in which case the result may be a worse attitude.

As our attitudes are often formed by external influences, individuals whose results are less than encouraging on this test may find it worth considering whether such influences are present in their lives. If these influences are negative, can the situation be changed so that any negative attitudes can be reversed?

A degree of self-analysis is often advantageous, as the more we understand about our own attitudes and beliefs the more chance we have of identifying and changing our negative attitudes to more positive ones.

Having the right attitude is increasingly important in modern living. When we buy goods, for example, we expect the person serving us to be enthusiastic and knowledgeable about the products he or she is selling, and at the same time eager to help and anxious to please the customer. It is this type of enthusiasm that people convey to others in all kinds of different situations.

| | |
|---|---|
| Total score 40–50 | Exceptionally high positive attitude factor |
| Total score 35–39 | High positive attitude factor |
| Total score 30–34 | Above average |
| Total score 25–29 | Average |
| Total score 20–24 | Below average |
| Total score 15–19 | Negative attitude factor |
| Total score 10–14 | Very negative attitude factor |
| Total score below 10 | Extremely negative attitude factor |

Transfer your score to the personality questionnaires overall assessment chart on page 153.

## Assessment for Test two

Award yourself 2 points for every 'b' answer, 1 point for every 'c', and 0 points for every 'a'.

## Analysis

Generally, success means achieving the things in life that we set out to achieve and the positive results of achieving this aim.

What is considered to be success by one individual may differ considerably for another. There is, therefore, no single definition or quantification of success. For many people success means being happy and secure, holding down a steady job to provide a regular income and providing for their family. For others, power, status and monetary wealth are their definition of success, and in a business environment they will not rest until they are at the top of the corporate ladder.

To whatever degree of success they aspire, successful people tend to set themselves targets or goals. These goals, which should provide meaningful yet realistic challenges, can be anything they want or need, and take them from where they are now to where they wish to be in the long-term or even short-term future.

It is necessary to strike the right balance in order to reach most of the goals we set out to achieve, both in our personal and in our working life. If we do not strike the right balance, then one part of our life is likely to suffer at the expense of another.

A keyword on the road to success is persistence. Most successful people overcome several hurdles before achieving their aspirations. It is important to view any setbacks positively and learn from them, quickly turning any losing situation into a winning one to regain control.

| | |
|---|---|
| Total score 40–50 | Exceptionally high positive success factor |
| Total score 35–39 | High positive success factor |
| Total score 30–34 | Above average |
| Total score 25–29 | Average |
| Total score 20–24 | Below average |
| Total score 15–19 | Negative success factor |
| Total score 10–14 | Very negative success factor |
| Total score below 10 | Extremely negative success factor |

Transfer your score to the personality questionnaires overall assessment chart on page 153.

## Assessment for Test three

Award yourself 2 points for every 'a' answer, 1 point for every 'c', and 0 points for every 'b'.

## Analysis

One definition of *imaginative* is 'bearing evidence of high creative force'.

People who are highly imaginative are, or have the potential to be, extremely creative and are not afraid of defying convention. In many walks of life, from music to architecture to literature, a high degree of imagination is necessary in order to produce great or original creations.

Although being highly imaginative is a tremendous asset and does enable some people to achieve great things, creative people may on occasions feel frustrated and dissatisfied that they have not achieved what they are capable of.

People who are highly imaginative also tend to be great thinkers. Each one of us has the potential to think more creatively, and we all have an imagination; it is just that some use it more than others. By allowing ourselves more thinking time, innovative ideas are more likely than not to start flowing. What people then do with these ideas is, of course, up to them, but without new inventive ideas no one is capable of achieving something original or exciting.

| | |
|---|---|
| Total score below 10 | Extremely negative imaginative factor |
| Total score 10–14 | Very negative imaginative factor |
| Total score 15–19 | Negative imaginative factor |
| Total score 20–24 | Below average |
| Total score 25–29 | Average |
| Total score 30–34 | Above average |
| Total score 35–39 | High positive imaginative factor |
| Total score 40–50 | Exceptionally high positive imaginative factor |

Transfer your score to the personality questionnaires overall assessment chart on page 153.

## Personality questionnaires: overall assessment

| Test | Description | Score |
|---|---|---|
| One | Attitude | |
| Two | Success factor | |
| Three | How imaginative are you? | |
| Total score | | |

A total of 150 points is available in this chapter. Divide your score by 3, round up to the nearest whole number and transfer the result to the overall brain quotient (BQ) rating chart on page 227.

# Tests and exercises of creative thinking

The term *creativity* refers to mental processes that lead to solutions, ideas, concepts, artistic forms, theories or products that are unique or novel.

Because it is underused, much creative talent in many people remains untapped throughout life. Until we try, most of us never know what we can actually achieve. We all have a creative side to our brain; therefore, we all have the potential to be creative. However, because of the pressures of modern living and the need for specialization in order to develop a successful career, many of us never have the time or opportunity, or indeed are given the encouragement, to explore our latent talents.

To be able to solve many problems involving creative thought processes it is often necessary to think laterally. The word *lateral* means 'of or relating to the side', 'away from the median axis'. Lateral thinking is a method of solving a problem by attempting to look at that problem from many angles rather than search for a direct head-on solution. It, therefore, involves the need to think outside the box and develop a degree of creative, innovative thinking, which seeks to change our natural and traditional perceptions, concepts and ideas. By developing this type of thinking we greatly increase our ability to solve problems that face us that we might not otherwise solve.

The term *thinking outside the box* was itself coined in the 1980s, when the four trees puzzle illustrated in Figure 7.1 was widely popular. The object of this puzzle is to draw four continuous straight lines, which must pass through all nine trees. Figure 7.2 shows the four-straight-line solution, in which it is necessary to draw the lines extending outside the square box of nine trees. Thus there is the need to think *outside the box* in order to achieve a solution, and the puzzle is a perfect example of the type of thinking necessary to solve many other similar puzzles and problems.

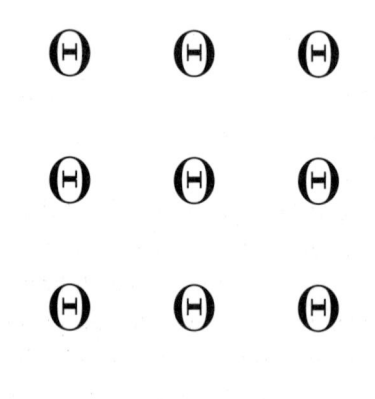

Figure 7.1

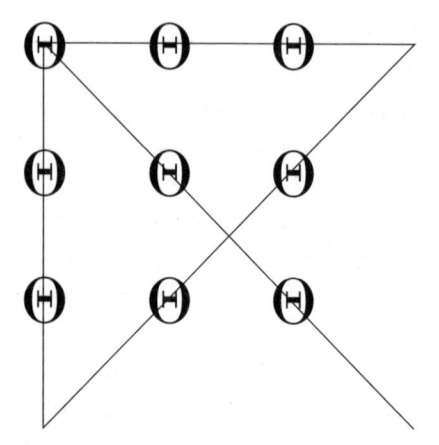

Figure 7.2

# PART 1: TESTS OF CREATIVE THINKING

The first part of this chapter consists of three tests, which are all timed and assessed.

## Test one: (symbolic) odd one out test

*Example:*
Which is the odd one out?

A. ♪ ● ○ □ ♣
B. ○ □ ♣ ♪ ●
C. □ ♣ ♪ ● ○
D. ♣ ♪ ○ ● □
E. ♣ ♪ ● ○ □

Answer: D.
Explanation: In all the others the five symbols are in the same order, albeit they start with a different symbol. Close inspection will reveal that the musical notation, ♪, is always followed by a black dot, ●. In D the musical notation, ♪, is followed by a white dot, ○.

You have 30 minutes in which to solve the 10 questions.

1. Which is the odd one out?

    A. ↑ → ← ↓ →
    B. ↓ ← → ↑ ←
    C. ↑ ← → → ↓
    D. ↓ → → ← ↑
    E. ↑ → ← → ↓

    Answer: ☐

2. Which is the odd one out?

   A. ♠ ♥ ♣ ♦ ♣
   B. ♠ ♥ ♣ ♠ ♦
   C. ♥ ♦ ♠ ♣ ♥
   D. ♠ ♥ ♣ ♦ ♣
   E. ♥ ♦ ♠ ♣ ♥

   Answer:

3. Which is the odd one out?

   A. ♫ √ Δ # ↑ √
   B. ○ □ ♂ ☺ ♪ →
   C. ┤ ┐ ┬ ⊥ ╬ ╚
   D. ☺ # ♫ ┤ □ ╚
   E. √ → ┐ # □ Δ

   Answer:

4. Which is the odd one out?

   A. ♫ → # ◄ Δ ╬ Σ
   B. ╚ — ╬ ▼ # ∏ ↕
   C. ◄ ▼ — ■ ▓ ╬ =
   D. ↕ ∏ # ▼ ╬ — ╚
   E. Σ ╬ Δ ◄ # → ♫

   Answer:

5. Which is the odd one out?

   A. = Σ Δ ◄ ♫ # ╬ □ ■
   B. ◄ ♫ # ╬ □ ■ = Σ Δ
   C. ♫ # ╬ □ ■ = Δ Σ ◄
   D. ╬ □ ■ = Σ Δ ◄ ♫ #
   E. □ ■ = Σ Δ ◄ ♫ # ╬

   Answer:

Tests and exercises of creative thinking

6. Which is the odd one out?

   A. → ↓ ↓ ← → ↓ ←
   B. ↓ → ← → ← ↓ →
   C. ← ↓ → ← ↓ ← ↓
   D. → ← → ← ↓ ← ↓
   E. → ← ↓ ↓ ← ↑ ←

   Answer: ☐

7. Which is the odd one out?

   A. ♪ = Σ Δ ◄ # 𝄐 → ▼
   B. Σ ♪ Δ ◄ = → # 𝄐 ▼
   C. = Δ # ◄ Σ ▼ ♪ → 𝄐
   D. 𝄐 Δ ◄ = ▼ ♪ Σ ♂ →
   E. = Δ ◄ # 𝄐 ♪ → ▼ Σ

   Answer: ☐

8. Which is the odd one out?

   A. ♪ ♯ □ ♣ ♪ → ☺ ← ◄ # ♂
   B. £ Ω ∏ & ♥ ♪ → ☺ ← ☼ □
   C. ♯ □ ♣ ♪ → ☺ ← ◄ # ♂ ∏
   D. ◄ # ♂ ☼ & ∏ ← ☺ → Ω £
   E. ♪ → ☺ ← ◄ # ♂ ☼ & ∏ ♪

   Answer: ☐

9. Which is the odd one out?

   A. ◄ ☼ ♣ ∏ ☼ Ω & # ♪
   B. $ ♪ ☺ ♂ ∏ Ω # ? @
   C. # @ ☺ ∏ $ ♪ Ω ♂ ?
   D. ☼ ◄ ♪ & Ω ♣ # ☼ ∏
   E. ☼ ? $ ☺ ◄ ♂ £ @ #

   Answer: ☐

10. Which is the odd one out?

A. ╬ ‖ ╠╤ ╚╬╣ ⊥
B. ╚╬=╣ ╬ ‖ ╠╤
C. ╣╬ ‖ ╠╤ ╚╬⊥
D. =╣╬ ‖ ╠╤ ╚╬
E. ‖╤ ╚╬=╣ ╬ ‖

Answer: ☐

# Test two: find the missing symbol test

In this test it is necessary to decide what sequence is occurring and work out, from the choice provided, what symbol or symbols are missing from within the sequence.

*Example:*
$ & ♠ ♀ • ♠ ♀ • $ & ♠ ♀ • $ & ♠ ♀ •

Which symbols below are missing from the above sequence?

A. ♠ ♀
B. & ♠
C. • $
D. $ &

Answer: D

Explanation: The sequence consists of the repeated symbols $ & ♠ ♀ •. The symbols $ & are, therefore, missing from the sequence, as indicated by the brackets:

$ & ♠ ♀ • ($ &) ♠ ♀ • $ & ♠ ♀ • $ & ♠ ♀ •

You have 40 minutes in which to solve the 10 questions.

1. ● ♀ ♥ ☺ ◘ ◄ ♪ ● ♀ ♥ ☺ ◘ ◄ ♀ ♥ ☺ ◘ ◄ ♪

   Which symbols below are missing from the above sequence?

   A. ◘ ◄
   B. ◄ ♪
   C. ♪ ●
   D. ♥ ☺

   Answer:

2. ≡ ∟ → ↔ ∥ ♥ & = ≡ ∟ → ♥ & =

   Which symbols below are missing from the above sequence?

   A. ↔ ∥
   B. ∥ ♥
   C. ∟ →
   D. ♥ &

   Answer:

3. ● ● ● ○ ○ ━ ● ● ○ ○ ━ ⬤ ● ● ● ○ ○ ━ ⬤

   Which symbols below are missing from the above sequence?

   A. ━ ●

   B. ● ○

   C. ━ ⬤

   D. ⬤ ●

   Answer:

4. ♪ • ≡ ‖ ♫ & ↔ ♪ ☺ ♠ • ≡ ‖ ♫ & ↔ ♪ ☺ ♠ • ≡ ‖ ♫ & ↔

   Which symbols below are missing from the above sequence?

   A. ☺ ♠
   B. ♪ ☺
   C. ↔ ♪
   D. ♪ •

   Answer: [        ]

5. ••••• ‖ •••• ‖ ••• ‖ •• ‖ • ‖ •••••• ‖ •••• ‖ ••• ‖ •• ‖ ••• •• ‖ •••• ‖ ••• ‖ •• ‖ • ‖

   Which symbols below are missing from the above sequence?

   A. ‖ ‖
   B. • ‖
   C. • •
   D. ‖ •

   Answer: [        ]

6. ⊓⊓ ⌐ ⊦⊣ ⌐ ⊓⊓ ⌐ ⊦⊣⊓ ⌐ ⊦⊣ ⌐ ⊓⊓ ⌐ ⊦⊣ ⌐

   Which symbols below are missing from the above sequence?

   A. ⊣ ⌐
   B. ⊓ ⌐
   C. ⌐ ⊓
   D. ⊓⊓

   Answer: [        ]

## Tests and exercises of creative thinking 163

7. ♠ ♥ ♦ ♣ ♥ ♦ ♣ ♠ ♥ ♦ ♣ ♥ ♦ ♣ ♠ ♦ ♣ ♦ ♣ ♠

   Which symbols below are missing from the above sequence?

   A. ♣ ♥
   B. ♠ ♠
   C. ♦ ♣
   D. ♠ ♥

   Answer: [ ]

8. ▲ ■ ◊ ▍– ♂ £ ↔ ∏ ▲ ■ ◊ ▍– ♂ £ ↔ ∏ ▲ ■ ◊ ▍– ♂ £ ↔
   ∏ ▲ ■ ◊ ♂ £ ↔ ∏ ▲ ■ ◊ ▍– ♂ £ ↔ ∏ ▲ ■ ◊ ▍– ♂ £ ↔ ∏

   Which symbols below are missing from the above sequence?

   A. ▍–
   B. ◊ ▍
   C. – ♂
   D. ▍∏

   Answer: [ ]

9. £ ¥ © « ® ¢ @ & $ # £ ¥ © « ® $ # £ ¥ © « ® ¢ @ & $

   Which symbols below are missing from the above sequence?

   A. # £ ¥
   B. ® ¢ @
   C. ¢ @ &
   D. & $ #

   Answer: [ ]

10. ■ □ ▫ ▫ ■ ▪ ▪ ▪ □ ▫ ▫ ▫ ▫ ■ ▪ ▪ ▪ ▪ ▪ ▪ □ ▫ ▫ ■ ▪ ▪ ▪ □ ▫ ▫ ▫ ■ ▪ ▪ ▪ □ ▫ ▫ ■ ▪ ▪ ▪ □ ▫ ▫ ▫ ▫ ■ ▪ ▪ ▪ ▪ ▪

Which symbols below are missing from the above sequence?

A. ■ ▪ ▪

B. ▫ ■ ■

C. ▪ □ ▫

D. ▫ ■ ▪

Answer: ⬚

# Test three: diagrammatic find the link test

Study the 10 diagrams below and use your imagination, powers of lateral thinking and knowledge to link the diagrams into five pairs. You have 20 minutes in which to complete the test.

## Answers to Test one

1. B. It contains two arrows facing west and one arrow facing east. All the rest contain two arrows facing east and one facing west.
2. B. A is the same as D, and C is the same as E.
3. A. It is the only one that contains a repeated symbol: √
4. C. A is E in reverse, and B is D in reverse.
5. C. The rest are all in the same order, albeit starting at a different symbol. In C, the two symbols Σ Δ are reversed: Δ Σ
6. E. It is the only one that contains an upward-pointing arrow.
7. D. All the rest contain the same nine symbols. D contains the symbol ♂ instead of the symbol #
8. D. In all the others the smiley face is preceded and followed by two arrows pointing towards it. In D it is the other way round.
9. E. A contains the same nine symbols as D, and B contains the same nine symbols as C.
10. A. The rest contain the same eight symbols in the same order, albeit starting with a different symbol each time. A reverses the symbols ⊥ ╣

## Assessment

Score 1 point for each correct answer.

| | |
|---|---|
| 4–5 | Average |
| 6–7 | Good |
| 8 | Very good |
| 9–10 | Exceptional |

Transfer your score to the tests of creative thinking overall assessment chart on page 168.

## Answers to Test two

1. C  2. A  3. D  4. A  5. B  6. C  7. D  8. A  9. C  10. D

## Assessment

Score 1 point for each correct answer.

| | |
|---|---|
| 4–5 | Average |
| 6–7 | Good |
| 8 | Very good |
| 9–10 | Exceptional |

Transfer your score to the tests of creative thinking overall assessment chart on page 168.

## Answers to Test three

1 and 6: The link is root (symbol for square root and root of a plant).
2 and 7: The link is chord (a set of notes is a chord, and the straight line joining two points on a circle's diameter is a chord).
3 and 10: The link is delta (a river delta and the Greek symbol delta).
4 and 5: The link is pie/pi (pie chart and symbol for the Greek letter pi).
8 and 9: The link is Taurus/torus (the astrological sign for Taurus and the torus ring-shaped surface).

## Assessment

Score 1 point for each pair of correct answers.

| | |
|---|---|
| 1–2 | Average |
| 3 | Good |
| 4 | Very good |
| 5 | Exceptional |

Transfer your score to the tests of creative thinking overall assessment chart on page 168.

# Tests of creative thinking: overall assessment

| Test | Description | Score |
|---|---|---|
| One | (Symbolic) odd one out test | |
| Two | Find the missing symbol test | |
| Three | Diagrammatic find the link test | |
| Total score | | |

A total of 25 points is available in this part.

| | |
|---|---|
| 10–13 | Average |
| 14–17 | Good |
| 18–22 | Very good |
| 23–25 | Exceptional |

Multiply your score by 2 and transfer the result to the overall brain quotient (BQ) rating chart on page 227.

# PART 2: EXERCISES OF CREATIVE THINKING

The second part of this chapter consists of three exercises all designed to explore and exercise your powers of creativity. As these are exercises only, the scores obtained will not contribute to your overall BQ rating.

## Brain hemispheres

The left-/right-brain thinking test contained in Exercise One is designed to explore left or right brain bias.

It was not until the mid-20th century that it was realized that every one of us has two sides to our brain, each side having different functions and characteristics. As a result of work carried out in the 1960s by the US neurologist Roger Wolcott Sperry (1913–94) it became apparent that the creative functions of human beings are controlled by the right-hand hemisphere of the human brain. This is the side of the brain that is underused by the majority of people, as opposed to the thought processes of the left-hand hemisphere, which is characterized by order, sequence and logic and is responsible for such functions as numerical and verbal skills.

Research begun in the 1950s had found that the cerebral cortex has two halves, called hemispheres, which are almost identical. These two brain hemispheres are connected by a bridge, or interface, of millions of nerve fibres called the corpus callosum that allows them to communicate with each other. The left side of the brain connects to the right side of the body, while the right side of the brain connects to the left side.

In the early 1960s Sperry and his team showed by a series of experiments, first using animals whose corpus callosum had been severed, and then on human patients whose corpus callosum had been severed in an attempt to cure epilepsy, that each of the two hemispheres has developed specialized functions and has its own private sensations, perceptions, ideas and thoughts, all separate from the opposite hemisphere.

As their experiments continued Sperry and his team were able to reveal much more about how the two hemispheres were specialized to perform different tasks. The left side of the brain is analytical and functions in a sequential and logical fashion and is the side that controls language, academic studies and rationality. The right side is creative and intuitive and leads, for example, to the birth of ideas for works of art and music.

While some individuals may be heavily weighted towards a particular hemisphere, this does not mean they are predominant in every one of that particular hemisphere's skills, since no one is entirely left- or right-brained. For example, whilst some individuals may have a strong overall bias towards left-side brain dominance, it may be that they still underperform on, for example, numerical tests and, therefore, need to work at that particular skill.

There is also always going to be an overlap between certain brain functions of opposing hemispheres, for example functions using logical processes and lateral thinking processes, where one is a predominantly right-brain function and the other is a predominantly left-brain function. However, when logical processes are being used the right brain does not switch off, and vice versa. On the contrary, both of these kinds of brain process work much more effectively when both sides of the brain are working together.

The importance to each of us of accessing both hemispheres of the brain is considerable. In order to support the whole-brain function, logic and intuition, to give just one example, are equally important.

## Exercise one: left-/right-brain thinking personality test

Below is a list of 40 words. Out of the 40 words choose only the 20 words that you believe are most applicable to yourself. Although there is no set time limit you should choose the 20 words as quickly and as intuitively as possible. If you are in any doubt as to the precise meaning of any of the words, the use of a dictionary is recommended.

At all times be completely honest and true to yourself with your answers in order to receive the most accurate assessment.

| | | | |
|---|---|---|---|
| stressed | thorough | thoughtful | submissive |
| inventive | bold | careless | frank |
| anxious | down-to-earth | visionary | businesslike |
| persistent | complex | flexible | concerned |
| sensible | methodical | emotional | intuitive |
| passive | realistic | analytical | intellectual |
| ruthless | artistic | disordered | content |
| patient | fanciful | habitual | unconventional |
| philosophical | curious | careful | rational |
| volatile | sensual | theoretical | organized |

## Analysis

*List A*
stressed
thorough
frank
submissive
down-to-earth
businesslike
persistent
sensible

*List B*
thoughtful
inventive
bold
careless
visionary
complex
flexible
concerned

| List A | List B |
|---|---|
| methodical | emotional |
| realistic | intuitive |
| analytical | passive |
| intellectual | artistic |
| ruthless | disordered |
| content | fanciful |
| patient | unconventional |
| habitual | philosophical |
| careful | curious |
| rational | volatile |
| organized | sensual |
| anxious | theoretical |

| | |
|---|---|
| 17 or more words selected in List A | Exceptionally high left-brain bias |
| 15–16 words selected in List A | High left-brain bias |
| 13–14 words selected in List A | Marked left-brain bias |
| 10–12 words selected in List A | No marked brain bias |
| 17 or more words selected in List B | Exceptionally high right-brain bias |
| 15–16 words selected in List B | High right-brain bias |
| 13–14 words selected in List B | Marked right-brain bias |
| 10–12 words selected in List B | No marked brain bias |

If the results of the above test indicate that you have a high right-brain bias you are likely to have a strongly intuitive and creative nature. However, if you have a strong left-side bias you are likely to be someone who is analytical and logical, with good numerical and verbal skills.

Although the advantages of having no brain bias considerably outweigh the disadvantages, one problem with hemispheric balance is that you may feel more inner conflict than someone with clearly established dominance. This conflict may be between what you feel and what you think. Sometimes details that seem important to the right hemisphere will be discounted by the left and vice versa, and this could prove a hindrance to an efficient learning process or the completion of tasks. On the positive side, having a balanced brain means that the learning and thinking process is likely to be enhanced when both sides of the brain work together in a balanced manner.

Balanced-brain individuals are also at an advantage when it comes to problem solving, as they are able to perceive the big picture and the essential details at the same time. Architects, for example, need to balance creativity with logic and detail in order to turn their concept into a workable, acceptable and economically viable reality.

Balanced-brain individuals also have the natural ability to succeed in multiple fields because of the great flexibility of mind that they possess.

## Exercise two: imaginative shapes

In each of the following use your imagination to create an original sketch or drawing of something recognizable incorporating the lines already provided. You have 30 minutes in which to complete the nine drawings.

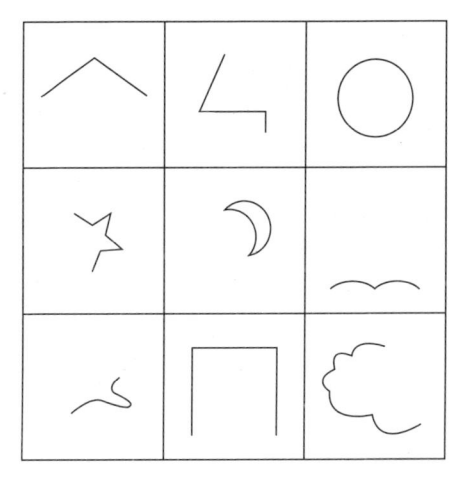

## Assessment

You can mark this test yourself. However, it is best marked by a friend or family member. Award 1 mark for each recognizable sketch, provided it is not similar to any of the other sketches. For example, if you draw a face, a second face scores no points, as each sketch must have an original theme. You thus obtain marks for variety. If you are creative, you will tend to try to draw something different for each sketch.

There is no one correct answer to any of the nine sketches, as for each there are any number of ideas.

| | |
|---|---|
| 3–4 | Average |
| 5–6 | Good |
| 7–8 | Very creative |
| 9 | Exceedingly creative |

Repeat the exercise as many times as you wish. Try other geometric objects or lines as a starting point.

## Exercise three: the bucket test

The following test is based on Gestalt and Jackson's test of divergent ability, which requires the subject to name as many new uses as possible for an object such as a bucket, a piece of cardboard or a paper clip.

In this test you are required to name as many uses as possible for a brick. Allow yourself six minutes to write up to 10 suggestions.

## Assessment

You can self-evaluate this test. However, it is best marked by a friend or family member. The following scores should be awarded:

- 2 points for any good, original or useful answer;
- 1 point for not-so-good answers that nevertheless constitute a good attempt;
- 0 points for completely impractical answers;
- 0 points for anti-social answers such as hitting someone over the head with the brick, or smashing a window in order to rob a jeweller's shop.

| | |
|---|---|
| 7–11 points | Average |
| 12–15 points | Creative |
| 16–20 points | Highly creative and imaginative mind |

# Memory

Memory is the process of storing and retrieving information in the brain. It is this process of memory that is central to our learning and thinking.

Human beings are continually learning throughout their lifetime. Only some of this massive volume of information is selected and stored in the brain, and is available for recall later when required. Learning is the acquisition of new knowledge, and memory is the retention of this knowledge. The combination of learning and memory, therefore, is the basis of all our knowledge and abilities. It is what enables us to consider the past, exist in the present and plan for the future. Its importance and power should not be underestimated.

Every part of our life relies to some extent on memory and is what enables us to walk, study, relax, communicate and play; in fact, whatever function we perform, some sort of memory process is at work.

While we have still much to learn about the physiology of memory storage in the brain, what is known is that memory involves the association of several brain systems working together. It is also accepted that the more we use our memory the better it becomes. It is, therefore, important to stimulate the memory by using it to the utmost, learning new skills and using memory-enhancing techniques.

The tests in this chapter are designed to test and assess your powers of memory and at the same time to assist you in improving your memory by developing your powers of concentration, and disciplining yourself to fix your mind on the subject being studied.

## Memory tests

1. This exercise tests your ability to remember pairs of words and form associations.

| CAMERA | CHICKEN | RIBBON |
| PEBBLE | CLOCK | ELEPHANT |
| | | |
| CHAIN | WHEEL | TRAMPOLINE |
| MOUSE | TRACTOR | LAMPPOST |
| | | |
| CHURCH | TREE | TELEPHONE |
| BEACH | WALLPAPER | ALSATION |
| | | |
| COMPUTER | TOWEL | MAGAZINE |
| YACHT | HOTEL | RIVER |

Study the 12 pairs of words for 10 minutes and use your imagination to link each pair of words shown above in as many ways as possible; then turn to page 180.

Question:
Put a letter A against one pair, the letter B against a second pair, etc, through to the letter L until you have matched what you think are the original 12 pairs of words:

| | |
|---|---|
| LAMPPOST | ............. |
| TREE | ............. |
| CAMERA | ............. |
| BEACH | ............. |
| MAGAZINE | ............. |
| COMPUTER | ............. |
| MOUSE | ............. |
| ELEPHANT | ............. |
| PEBBLE | ............. |
| RIBBON | ............. |
| TELEPHONE | ............. |
| CHICKEN | ............. |
| CHURCH | ............. |
| RIVER | ............. |
| CHAIN | ............. |
| TOWEL | ............. |
| YACHT | ............. |
| TRACTOR | ............. |
| TRAMPOLINE | ............. |
| CLOCK | ............. |
| WHEEL | ............. |
| HOTEL | ............. |
| ALSATION | ............. |
| WALLPAPER | ............. |

2.

|  $  |  ¢  |
|-----|-----|
|  £  |  ¥  |

Study the above for 10 seconds; then wait for five minutes before turning to page 182.

Question:
Which one of the following did you look at five minutes ago?

| $ | ¢ | | ¢ | £ | | $ | ¢ | | ¢ | $ | | $ | £ |
|---|---|---|---|---|---|---|---|---|---|---|---|---|---|
| ¥ | £ | | ¥ | $ | | £ | ¥ | | £ | ¥ | | ¥ | ¢ |
| A | | | B | | | C | | | D | | | E | |

Answer: [ ]

3.

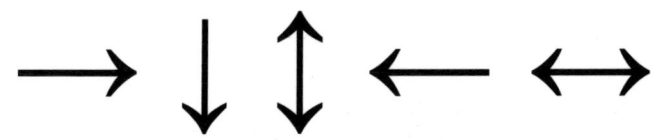

$$\rightarrow \quad \downarrow \quad \updownarrow \quad \leftarrow \quad \leftrightarrow$$

Study the above for 20 seconds and then turn straight to page 184.

Question:
Which of the following have you just looked at?

1. ← ↑ ↔ ↑ →
2. ↑ ↓ ↔ ↑ →
3. → ↕ ↑ → ↔
4. → ↓ ↕ ← ↔
5. → ↑ ↕ ← ↔

Answer: ☐

4. Try to memorize the rows of figures in five minutes; then turn straight to page 186.

2 4 6 7 3 9 1
7 9 1 6 8 5 2
5 6 3 8 9 2 6
9 3 7 4 5 1 2
6 5 9 3 4 7 1

Questions:

a. What are the first two digits on the top row?

Answer: ☐

b. Which is the only number that appears in every row of figures?

Answer: ☐

c. What is the final number on the bottom row?

Answer: ☐

d. Which is the only number to appear twice on the same row?

Answer: ☐

5.  𝄀 ☺ ¥ Ω ◀ ♪ ♠ #

Study the above set of symbols for one minute; then wait for one minute and turn to page 188.

Questions:

⊣| ☺ € ¥ ♪ ◀ Ω ♠ #

i.  Which two symbols have changed places?

Answer: [　　　]

ii. Which new symbol has been introduced?

Answer: [　　　]

6. Study the following, which is an extract from a diary for 13 days in October, for five minutes; then turn straight to page 192.

| Date | Morning | Afternoon | Evening |
|---|---|---|---|
| Monday 3 | | Business meeting with Wonky Gizmo Company Ltd 3.30 | |
| Tuesday 4 | Sales conference 9.30 | | |
| Wednesday 5 | | Phone Barry | Bowling 8.30 |
| Thursday 6 | | | Dinner with Jane and Robert 8.30 |
| Friday 7 | Dental appointment 10.30 | | |
| Saturday 8 | | Golf tournament 1.30 | |
| Sunday 9 | | | |
| Monday 10 | Pick up Mr and Mrs Lawson from train station 11.30 | | |

*continued on page 190*

| Date | Morning | Afternoon | Evening |
|---|---|---|---|
| Tuesday 11 | | Phone Ben | |
| Wednesday 12 | Mum and Dad's 40th wedding anniversary | | |
| Thursday 13 | | | Leaving presentation party for Christine 7.30 |
| Friday 14 | | Collect hire car 2.30 | |
| Saturday 15 | | | Prepare papers for Monday's meeting with Japanese customers |

Questions:

i. The diary covers 13 days during which month?

Answer: [          ]

ii. What wedding anniversary will be celebrated on Wednesday 12th?

Answer: [          ]

iii. What time is the dental appointment on Friday 7th?

Answer: [          ]

iv. With whom, on Thursday 6th, is the dinner date?

Answer: [          ]

v. What function is scheduled for Thursday 13th?

Answer: [          ]

vi. When am I due to collect the hire car?

Answer: [          ]

vii. Which is the only day on which two diary entries are made?

Answer: [          ]

viii. Who am I scheduled to pick up from the train station on Monday 10th?

Answer: [          ]

ix. What will I be doing at 1.30 on Saturday 8th?

Answer: [          ]

x. Who must I telephone in the afternoon of Wednesday 5th?

Answer: ☐

xi. With whom do I have a meeting on Monday 3rd?

Answer: ☐

xii. What must I do on the evening of Saturday 15th?

Answer: ☐

xiii. Name the day, date and time for my dental appointment.

Answer: ☐

xiv. Which is the only day when I have no diary entry?

Answer: ☐

xv. What time is my business meeting on Monday 3rd?

Answer: ☐

7. Study the fictitious address below for two minutes:

Carl Peters
The Willows
5th Floor
94 Grand Beech Road
Cippenham
Wiltshire
WJ19 8FX

Now wait for two minutes; then turn to page 196.

Question:
Now try to fill in the gaps correctly:

Carl ........................

The ............................................

..... th Floor

94 ..................... Beech ..........................

Cippenham

.............................................

WJ ...... 8 .......

8. Study the set of figures below for one minute; then turn straight to page 198.

♠ 9 ▶ 4 W ♪ Ω 5 ☐ $ 4 Ω 8

Questions:

i. Which symbol appears in the set twice?

Answer:

ii. Which number appears in the set twice?

Answer:

9.

|   |   |   |
|---|---|---|
| O | O | X |
| X | O | X |
| X | X | O |

Study the above for 20 seconds and then turn straight to page 200.

Question:
Which of the following have you just looked at?

|   | 1 |   |   | 2 |   |   | 3 |   |
|---|---|---|---|---|---|---|---|---|
| X | X | O | O | O | X | O | X | O |
| X | O | X | X | O | X | O | X | X |
| O | X | X | O | X | X | X | X | O |

| X | O | X | O | O | X | O | X | O |
|---|---|---|---|---|---|---|---|---|
| X | X | O | X | O | X | X | O | X |
| O | O | X | X | X | O | O | O | X |
|   | 4 |   |   | 5 |   |   | 6 |   |

Answer: [ ]

10.

|   | $ |   | 2 |
|---|---|---|---|
|   | 3 |   | ↑ |
|   |   | & | f |
| m |   |   |   |

Study the above for one minute; then turn straight to page 202.

Questions:

a. The arrow is pointing to which number?

Answer: [ ]

b. What letter appears immediately to the right of the ampersand (&)?

Answer: [ ]

c. What letter appears in the bottom left-hand corner?

Answer: [ ]

d. What number appears immediately below the dollar ($) symbol?

Answer: [ ]

## Assessment

Score 1 point for each correct pair of answers in question 1 and 1 point for each correct answer in the remaining questions. A total of 50 points is available in this chapter.

| | |
|---|---|
| 16–24 | Average |
| 25–34 | Good |
| 35–44 | Very good |
| 45–50 | Exceptional |

Transfer your score to the overall brain quotient (BQ) rating chart on page 227.

# Tests of verbal aptitude

Mastery of words is seen by many as having in one's possession the ability to produce order out of chaos, and as a result it is argued by many that command of vocabulary is a true and accurate measure of intelligence.

The puzzles and tests in this chapter are designed to measure and strengthen the basic ability to understand and use words, and they include word meanings, synonyms and antonyms.

## Test one: synonym test

A synonym is a word having a similar meaning to another in the same language. For example, synonyms of the word *correct* are, in one sense, *accurate* and *exact*, in another sense *amend* and *rectify* and, in yet another sense, *admonish* and *chastise*. You have 45 minutes in which to answer the 30 questions.

1. Which word in brackets is closest in meaning to the word in capitals?

    NATURE
    (basics, duty, personality, clarity, phenomena)

    Answer:

2. Which word in brackets is closest in meaning to the word in capitals?

   ROUT
   (procedure, defeat, itinerary, tame, rebel)

   Answer:

3. Which word in brackets is closest in meaning to the word in capitals?

   ASSERTIVE
   (willing, inquiring, dogmatic, unreasonable, stubborn)

   Answer:

4. Which word in brackets is closest in meaning to the word in capitals?

   SUCCINCT
   (eminent, pithy, indistinct, prolix, turgid)

   Answer:

5. Which word in brackets is closest in meaning to the word in capitals?

   SURROUNDINGS
   (air, environment, pacific, circle, flora)

   Answer:

6. Which word in brackets is closest in meaning to the word in capitals?

   PROPITIATORY
   (opportune, conciliatory, comparable, apt, trite)

   Answer:

7. Which word in brackets is closest in meaning to the word in capitals?

   SENSATION
   (wish, decision, feeling, hope, appreciation)

   Answer:

8. Which word in brackets is closest in meaning to the word in capitals?

   SEMINAL
   (benchmark, academic, literal, similar, independent)

   Answer:

9. Which word in brackets is closest in meaning to the word in capitals?

   HELM
   (steer, root, tilt, control, deck)

   Answer:

10. Which word in brackets is closest in meaning to the word in capitals?

    VESTIGIAL
    (seasoned, habitual, dark, underdeveloped, passage)

    Answer:

11. Which word in brackets is closest in meaning to the word in capitals?

    WASPISH
    (sharp, cantankerous, busy, profligate, insipid)

    Answer:

12. Which word in brackets is closest in meaning to the word in capitals?

    BROILING
    (bubbling, arguing, swelling, springing, torrid)

    Answer:

13. Which two words are closest in meaning?

    infinite, clear, flaccid, limpid, sweet, supple

    Answer:

14. Which two words are closest in meaning?

    dubious, token, manifest, pointer, nominal, diverse

    Answer:

15. Which two words are closest in meaning?

    factory, pound, enclosure, site, work, destroy

    Answer:

16. Which two words are closest in meaning?

    thwart, titillate, collapse, smack, instil, frustrate

    Answer:

17. Which two words are closest in meaning?

    pressing, argent, vocation, silver, vernacular, previous

    Answer:

18. Which two words are closest in meaning?

    tactless, careless, indelicate, stagnant, liberal, impolite

    Answer: [          ]

19. Which two words are closest in meaning?

    insensitive, blithe, naive, cheerful, virtuous, bold

    Answer: [          ]

20. Which two words are closest in meaning?

    compact, subtle, diminished, delicate, reciprocal, informal

    Answer: [          ]

21. Which two words are closest in meaning?

    punishing, fastidious, dilapidated, piercing, remorseful, meticulous

    Answer: [          ]

22. Which two words are closest in meaning?

    rural, sylvan, figurative, uniform, pleasant, romantic

    Answer: [          ]

23. Which two words are closest in meaning?

    intervene, waive, signify, renounce, move, pause

    Answer: [          ]

24. Which two words are closest in meaning?

    synergy, franchise, dynamism, interaction, compendium, eternity

    Answer:

25. Which two words are closest in meaning?

    dispute, attest, certify, minister, fulfil, appoint

    Answer:

26. Which two words are most similar in meaning to the phrase HANG IN THERE?

    cooperate, persevere, clutch, endure, preserve, relax

    Answer:

27. Which two words are most similar in meaning to the phrase PUT TWO AND TWO TOGETHER?

    explain, deduce, convince, accomplish, conclude, finalize

    Answer:

28. Which two words are most similar in meaning to the phrase LAID BACK?

    prostrate, casual, tolerant, indisposed, unrestrained, friendly

    Answer:

29. Which two words are most similar in meaning to the phrase PINCH OF SALT?

    cautiously, brackish, sceptically, poignantly, seasonally, economically

    Answer:

30. Which two words are most similar in meaning to the phrase TAKE INTO CONSIDERATION?

    enumerate, study, enlist, heed, adopt, surmise

    Answer:

## Test two: antonym test

An antonym is a word with the opposite meaning to another in the same language. For example the word *big* is opposite to the word *small*, the word *true* is opposite to the word *false*, and the word *happy* is opposite to the word *sad*. You have 45 minutes in which to answer the 30 questions.

1.  Which word in brackets is most opposite in meaning to the word in capitals?

    INVOLVED
    (concerned, elementary, parted, injudicious, indistinct)

    Answer:

2.  Which word in brackets is most opposite in meaning to the word in capitals?

    PLIABLE
    (susceptible, stubborn, hard, limber, tough)

    Answer:

3. Which word in brackets is most opposite in meaning to the word in capitals?

   EQUIVOCAL
   (different, definite, prone, vague, unbalanced)

   Answer:

4. Which word in brackets is most opposite in meaning to the word in capitals?

   RUEFUL
   (delighted, gracious, pallid, penitent, relaxed)

   Answer:

5. Which word in brackets is most opposite in meaning to the word in capitals?

   TACTICAL
   (garrulous, unclear, blundering, circuitous, explicit)

   Answer:

6. Which word in brackets is most opposite in meaning to the word in capitals?

   BANAL
   (platitudinous, permissive, challenging, harmful, impartial)

   Answer:

7. Which word in brackets is most opposite in meaning to the word in capitals?

   CURSORILY
   (somewhat, politely, thoroughly, diplomatically, adequately)

   Answer:

8. Which two words below are most opposite to the phrase RUN OF THE MILL?

   fair, marvellous, healthy, unusual, vigorous, impulsive

   Answer: [          ]

9. Which word in brackets is most opposite in meaning to the word in capitals?

   CUMBERSOME
   (loose, shrewd, wieldy, pithy, innocent)

   Answer: [          ]

10. Which word in brackets is most opposite in meaning to the word in capitals?

    AGOG
    (calm, clumsy, apathetic, quiet, sultry, listless)

    Answer: [          ]

11. Which word in brackets is most opposite in meaning to the word in capitals?

    EXUBERANT
    (energetic, slow, subdued, withdrawn, adverse)

    Answer: [          ]

12. Which word in brackets is most opposite in meaning to the word in capitals?

    MELODIOUS
    (euphonious, soft, discordant, expansive, loud)

    Answer: [          ]

13. Which word in brackets is most opposite in meaning to the word in capitals?

    IMMINENT
    (static, remote, threatening, controlled, estimable)

    Answer:

14. Which word in brackets is most opposite in meaning to the word in capitals?

    ILLIBERAL
    (tolerant, licit, affable, uncharitable, conservative)

    Answer:

15. Which word in brackets is most opposite in meaning to the word in capitals?

    LOGICAL
    (peculiar, irrational, difficult, protracted, incorrect)

    Answer:

16. Which two words are most opposite in meaning?

    counteract, nurture, acclaim, ignore, advise, transmit

    Answer:

17. Which two words are most opposite in meaning?

    moderate, majestic, fine, humble, authentic, neurotic

    Answer:

18. Which two words are most opposite in meaning?

    laud, downgrade, adjust, better, carry, create

    Answer:

19. Which two words are most opposite in meaning?

    expensive, reverent, expansive, disrespectful, reticent, candid

    Answer:

20. Which two words are most opposite in meaning?

    annihilate, hasten, create, entreat, defeat, climb

    Answer:

21. Which two words are most opposite in meaning?

    energetic, consistent, sporting, unfair, tawdry, glorious

    Answer:

22. Which two words are most opposite in meaning?

    balmy, stark, sensible, stormy, prejudiced, snug

    Answer:

23. Which two words are most opposite in meaning?

    biased, objective, regrettable, optimal, incorrect, unreasonable

    Answer:

24. Which two words are most opposite in meaning?

    luxurious, solid, palatable, florid, tasteless, severe

    Answer: [          ]

25. Which two words are most opposite in meaning?

    grateful, prosaic, modern, fascinating, flourishing, catastrophic

    Answer: [          ]

26. Which two words below are most opposite in meaning to the phrase FEW AND FAR BETWEEN?

    veracious, manifold, curving, abundant, manifest, spurious

    Answer: [          ]

27. Which two words are most opposite in meaning?

    simple, brisk, enervating, transparent, oppressive, regular

    Answer: [          ]

28. Which two words are most opposite in meaning?

    imagine, cede, surmise, arrange, concentrate, disperse

    Answer: [          ]

29. Which two words are most opposite in meaning?

    prolong, drawback, formulate, berate, collection, asset

    Answer: [          ]

30. Which two words are most opposite in meaning?

   lionization, exaggeration, review, restraint, outcry, fabrication

   Answer: [          ]

# Test three: synonym and antonym test

In each of the following select two words that are synonyms, plus an antonym of these two synonyms, from the list of words given. You have 20 minutes in which to complete the 10 questions.

1. ban, betray, proscribe, authorize, indict, chaperone

   Answers: [          ]

2. hasty, isolated, recurrent, prejudiced, responsive, continued

   Answers: [          ]

3. pliable, deliberate, tenacious, impulsive, studied, solid

   Answers: [          ]

4. liable, innocent, legal, edifying, culpable, devious

   Answers: [          ]

5. maintain, evoke, reform, restate, recant, decline

   Answers: [          ]

6. ambiguous, unequivocal, expert, hesitant, unskilful, unclear

   Answers: [          ]

7. brief, latent, hitherto, hidden, punctual, evident

   Answers: [                    ]

8. few, limited, copious, numerous, finite, microscopic

   Answers: [                    ]

9. anticlimax, purifier, letdown, remedy, culmination, pollutant

   Answers: [                    ]

10. supporter, patron, acquaintance, adversary, counterpart, beneficiary

    Answers: [                    ]

## Test four: lexical ability test

This test consists of three types of question, each designed to test a different aspect of your lexical ability. The question types are as follows:

- *Type 1.* You are given the first part of a word or phrase and you have to find the second part. This second part then becomes the first part of the second word or phrase, for example: back (     ) breaking. The word *ground* would then complete the word back*ground*, and the word *ground* would also commence the phrase *ground*-breaking.
- *Type 2.* This set of questions is designed to test the ability to find alternative meanings of words. In each case you are looking for a word having the same meanings as the two definitions provided. For example: travelling entertainment (     ) free from discrimination. The word you are looking for is *fair*, which means the same as the definition on the left-

hand side of the brackets in one sense and the same as the definition on the right-hand side in another sense.

- *Type 3.* These questions are designed to test knowledge of word meanings and spelling ability by identifying letter patterns from which to construct a nine-letter word with the aid of the definition provided. In each case you are given nine three-letter bits and must identify the correct three three-letter bits in order to produce the nine-letter word. For example the word *haphazard* consists of the three three-letter bits *hap*, *haz*, *ard*.

You have 90 minutes in which to solve the 30 questions.

*Questions 1–10 (Type 1):*
Insert a word in the brackets so that it completes a word or phrase when tacked on to the word on the left and completes another word or phrase when placed in front of the word on the right.

1. EVER (     ) OVER     Answer:

2. MELT (     ) RIGHT     Answer:

3. WHOLE (     ) PRICE     Answer:

4. RAM (     ) RIDGE     Answer:

5. DRY (     ) CUT     Answer:

6. FAIR (     ) PLAN     Answer:

7. COPY (      ) ANGLE

    Answer:

8. BACK (      ) LET

    Answer:

9. ROCK (      ) OUT

    Answer:

10. FREE (      ) MARK

    Answer:

*Questions 11–20 (Type 2):*
Place a word in the brackets that means the same as the definitions outside the brackets.

11. rubbish (      ) the offspring at one birth

    Answer:

12. stem (      ) track

    Answer:

13. compartment in a stable (      ) come to a standstill

    Answer:

14. illuminate (      ) alleviate

    Answer:

15. brawl (      ) fragment

    Answer:

16. sudden attack (      ) accuse formally

    Answer:

17. fox's tail (        ) skirmish

    Answer: [        ]

18. section of a canal (        ) fastening device

    Answer: [        ]

19. part of the hand (        ) type of tree

    Answer: [        ]

20. average (        ) stingy

    Answer: [        ]

*Questions 21–30 (Type 3):*

21. Place three of the nine three-letter bits together to produce a word meaning THE SKY OR HEAVENS.

    ATE  PED  ENT  MAM  VEN  BER  DIS  EIN  FIR

    Answer: [        ]

22. Place three of the nine three-letter bits together to produce a word meaning INCLINED TO SLEEP.

    FUL  NOL  BER  DAY  ENT  TER  PAN  SOM  OUR

    Answer: [        ]

23. Place three of the nine three-letter bits together to produce a word meaning ATTENDANTS OR ASSOCIATES.

    NEL  VIS  ENT  CLO  AGE  FIN  GRA  OUR  GES

    Answer: [        ]

24. Place three of the nine three-letter bits together to produce a word meaning GENERAL AGREEMENT.

    OTH   SEN   ENT   PLI   SUS   ACT   CON   TER   PIN

    Answer: _____

25. Place three of the nine three-letter bits together to produce a word meaning FULL OF JUICE.

    RYT   CUL   TLE   ENT   SUC   ELA   IST   PAT   AWL

    Answer: _____

26. Place three of the nine three-letter bits together to produce a word meaning PRAISEWORTHY.

    EDI   TER   IRA   MOD   ADM   ECT   CUL   PLY   BLE

    Answer: _____

27. Place three of the nine three-letter bits together to produce a word meaning WITHOUT FLEXIBILITY.

    SED   TIC   BUN   INE   EAR   CEI   LAS   GES   OSE

    Answer: _____

28. Place three of the nine three-letter bits together to produce a word meaning SHORT-LIVED.

    LET   RUE   EME   TLE   BNO   EPH   IND   WIL   RAL

    Answer: _____

29. Place three of the nine three-letter bits together to produce a word meaning AN INTRICATE, COMPLICATED PLOT.

    ROG   AND   TER   INC   IMB   ATE   KLE   LIO   END

    Answer: [　　　　　　　　　]

30. Place three of the nine three-letter bits together to produce a word meaning MAKE EASIER.

    ALL   ITE   NFL   ENT   EVI   ATE   NIM   LOG   STE

    Answer: [　　　　　　　　　]

## Answers to Test one

1. personality 2. defeat 3. dogmatic 4. pithy 5. environment 6. conciliatory 7. feeling 8. benchmark 9. control 10. underdeveloped 11. cantankerous 12. torrid 13. clear, limpid 14. token, nominal 15. pound, enclosure 16. thwart, frustrate 17. argent, silver 18. tactless, impolite 19. blithe, cheerful 20. subtle, delicate 21. fastidious, meticulous 22. rural, sylvan 23. waive, renounce 24. synergy, interaction 25. attest, certify 26. persevere, endure 27. deduce, conclude 28. casual, tolerant 29. cautiously, sceptically 30. study, heed

## Assessment

Score 1 point for each correct answer.

|  |  |
| --- | --- |
| 12–17 | Average |
| 18–23 | Good |
| 24–27 | Very good |
| 28–30 | Exceptional |

Transfer your score to the tests of verbal aptitude overall assessment chart on page 225.

## Answers to Test two

1. elementary 2. stubborn 3. definite 4. delighted 5. blundering 6. challenging 7. thoroughly 8. marvellous, unusual 9. wieldy 10. apathetic 11. subdued 12. discordant 13. remote 14. tolerant 15. irrational 16. nurture, ignore 17. majestic, humble 18. downgrade, better 19. reverent, disrespectful 20. annihilate, create 21. sporting, unfair 22. balmy, stormy 23. biased, objective 24. palatable, tasteless 25. prosaic, fascinating 26. manifold, abundant 27. brisk, enervating 28. concentrate, disperse 29. drawback, asset 30. exaggeration, restraint

## Assessment

Score 1 point for each correct answer.

| | |
|---|---|
| 12–17 | Average |
| 18–23 | Good |
| 24–27 | Very good |
| 28–30 | Exceptional |

Transfer your score to the tests of verbal aptitude overall assessment chart on page 225.

## Answers to Test three

1. Synonyms: ban, proscribe. Antonym: authorize
2. Synonyms: recurrent, continued. Antonym: isolated
3. Synonyms: deliberate, studied. Antonym: impulsive
4. Synonyms: liable, culpable. Antonym: innocent
5. Synonyms: maintain, restate. Antonym: recant
6. Synonyms: ambiguous, unclear. Antonym: unequivocal
7. Synonyms: hidden, latent. Antonym: evident
8. Synonyms: copious, numerous. Antonym: few
9. Synonyms: anticlimax, letdown. Antonym: culmination
10. Synonyms: patron, supporter. Antonym: adversary

## Assessment

Score 1 point for each correct answer.

| | |
|---|---|
| 4–5 | Average |
| 6–7 | Good |
| 8 | Very good |
| 9–10 | Exceptional |

Transfer your score to the tests of verbal aptitude overall assessment chart on page 225.

## Answers to Test four

1. more 2. down 3. sale 4. part 5. clean 6. game 7. right 8. drop 9. bottom 10. trade (or speech or post) 11. litter 12. stalk 13. stall 14. lighten 15. scrap 16. charge 17. brush 18. lock 19. palm 20. mean 21. firmament 22. somnolent 23. entourage 24. consensus 25. succulent 26. admirable 27. inelastic 28. ephemeral 29. imbroglio 30. alleviate

## Assessment

Score 1 point for each correct answer.

| | |
|---|---|
| 12–17 | Average |
| 18–23 | Good |
| 24–27 | Very good |
| 28–30 | Exceptional |

Transfer your score to the tests of verbal aptitude overall assessment chart on page 225.

# Tests of verbal aptitude: overall assessment

| Test | Description | Score |
|---|---|---|
| One | Synonym test | |
| Two | Antonym test | |
| Three | Synonym and antonym test | |
| Four | Lexical ability test | |
| Total score | | |

A total of 100 points is available in this chapter.

| | |
|---|---|
| 32–48 | Average |
| 49–78 | Good |
| 79–88 | Very good |
| 89–100 | Exceptional |

Divide your score by 2, round up to the nearest whole number and transfer the result to the overall brain quotient (BQ) rating chart on page 227.

# 10

# Overall BQ rating and assessment

You should enter each total transferable score, as instructed, from the end of each chapter into the overall BQ rating chart below to obtain your final brain quotient (BQ) rating factor.

| Chapter | Description | Total score |
|---|---|---|
| 1 | IQ testing | |
| 2 | Agility of mind | |
| 3 | Tests of logical analysis | |
| 4 | Tests of numerical aptitude | |
| 5 | Tests of spatial aptitude | |
| 6 | Personality questionnaires | |
| 7 | Tests of creative thinking | |
| 8 | Memory tests | |
| 9 | Tests of verbal aptitude | |
| Final BQ rating | | |

## Overall brain quotient (BQ) assessment

Maximum number of points available: 450.

| Final BQ rating | Assessment |
| --- | --- |
| BQ below 50 | Very low |
| BQ 51–100 | Low |
| BQ 101–149 | Borderline low |
| BQ 150–189 | Low average |
| BQ 190–249 | Middle average |
| BQ 250–314 | High average |
| BQ 315–359 | High |
| BQ 360–389 | Very high |
| BQ 390–450 | Exceptional |

## Analysis

In addition to the above BQ assessment, it is suggested you analyse your performance for each of the nine chapters. An analysis of individual scores in each of these chapters will enable you to identify any areas of strengths and weaknesses and provide you with the opportunity of building and capitalizing on your strengths and at the same time of working on improving your performance in areas of weakness.

As well as the identifying of such strengths and weaknesses, the tests and exercises in this book perform another important function, that of using and exercising the brain. In order continually to increase and maximize our brainpower, there is a need constantly to work out our brains in order to strengthen performance.

It is important that we continually stimulate our brains. For example, the more we practise at tests of verbal aptitude the more we increase our ability to understand the meaning of words and use them effectively; the more we practise at mathematics the more confident we become when working with numbers; and the more we practise our ability to move our fingers and manipulate small objects, the more dextrous we become at operations involving this type of aptitude.

The brain is undoubtedly our greatest asset, yet for many of us it is the part of the body we take most for granted. Our brain needs care and exercise in the same way as other parts of the body. We eat the right foods to keep our heart healthy and we moisturize our skin to keep it from drying out. However, just as gymnasts strive to increase their performance at whatever level they are competing by means of punishing training schedules and refinement of technique, there are exercises, or mental gymnastics, we can do to increase the performance of the brain and enhance quickness of thought.

By continually exploiting our enormous brain potential we have the ability to make more and stronger connections between our nerve cells, with the result that not only our mental but also our physical long-term well-being will benefit.

# ALSO AVAILABLE FROM KOGAN PAGE

**HOW TO PASS ADVANCED VERBAL REASONING TESTS**
Essential practice for English usage, critical reasoning and reading comprehension tests
MIKE BRYON
ISBN: 978 0 7494 4969 8
Paperback 2008

**HOW TO PASS ADVANCED NUMERACY TESTS**
Revised edition
Improve your scores in numerical reasoning and data interpretation psychometric tests
MIKE BRYON
ISBN: 978 0 7494 5229 2
Paperback 2008

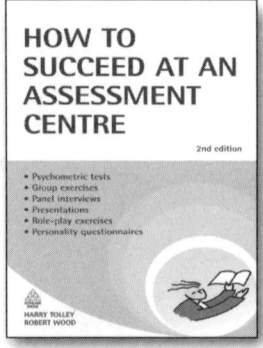

**HOW TO SUCCEED AT AN ASSESSMENT CENTRE**
2nd edition
- Psychometric tests
- Group exercises
- Panel interviews
- Presentations
- Role-play exercises
- Personality questionnaires

HARRY TOLLEY
ROBERT WOOD
ISBN: 978 0 7494 4421 1
Paperback 2005

**TEST YOUR NUMERICAL APTITUDE**
How to assess your numeracy skills and plan your career
JIM BARRETT
ISBN: 978 0 7494 5064 9
Paperback 2007

Order online now at www.koganpage.com

Sign up for regular e-mail updates on new Kogan Page books in your interest area

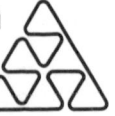

# ALSO AVAILABLE FROM KOGAN PAGE

**IQ AND PSYCHOMETRIC TESTS**
Second edition
Assess your personality, aptitude and intelligence
PHILIP CARTER

ISBN-13: 978 0 7494 5106 6
Paperback 2007

**HOW TO PASS GRADUATE PSYCHOMETRIC TESTS**
3rd edition
Over 500 practice questions
Essential preparation for numerical and verbal ability tests plus personality questionnaires
MIKE BRYON

ISBN: 978 0 7494 4852 3
Paperback 2007

**IQ and Personality Tests**
Assess and improve your creativity, aptitude and intelligence
PHILIP CARTER

ISBN: 978 0 7494 4954 4
Paperback 2007

**HOW TO MASTER PSYCHOMETRIC TESTS**
Expert advice on test preparation with practice questions from leading test publishers
MARK PARKINSON

ISBN: 978 0 7494 5165 3
Paperback 2008

Order online now at www.koganpage.com

Sign up for regular e-mail updates on new Kogan Page books in your interest area

# ALSO AVAILABLE FROM KOGAN PAGE

**CAREER, APTITUDE & SELECTION TESTS**
2nd edition
INTERMEDIATE LEVEL
Match your IQ, personality & abilities to your ideal career
JIM BARRETT

ISBN: 978 0 7494 4819 6
Paperback 2006

**IQ AND APTITUDE TESTS**
Assess your verbal, numerical, and spatial reasoning skills
PHILIP CARTER

ISBN: 978 0 7494 4931 5
Paperback 2007

**THE APTITUDE TEST WORKBOOK**
Revised edition
Discover your potential and improve your career options with practice psychometric tests
JIM BARRETT

ISBN: 978 0 7494 5237 7
Paperback 2008

**TEST YOUR OWN APTITUDE**
3rd edition
INTERMEDIATE LEVEL
New updated edition of the best-selling guide
JIM BARRETT
GEOFF WILLIAMS

ISBN: 978 0 7494 3887 6
Paperback 2003

Order online now at www.koganpage.com

Sign up for regular e-mail updates on new Kogan Page books in your interest area